The Complete
Job Interview Handbook

THE COMPLETE JOB INTERVIEW HANDBOOK

THIRD EDITION

JOHN J. MARCUS

 HarperPerennial
A Division of HarperCollins*Publishers*

HarperCollins books may be purchased for educational, business, or sales promotional use. For information, please write to: Special Markets Department, HarperCollins Publishers, Inc., 10 East 53rd Street, New York, NY 10022.

Library of Congress Cataloging-in-Publication Data

Marcus, John J.
    Complete job interview handbook / by John Marcus.—3rd ed.
       p.   cm.
    Includes index.
    ISBN 0-06-273266-8
    1. Employment interviewing. I. Title.
HF5549.5.I6M315   1994
650.14—dc20   93-42353

97 98 ❖/HC 10 9 8

To Laurie—love of my life.

"The winds and waves are always on the side of the ablest navigators."

—EDWARD GIBBON,
THE DECLINE AND FALL OF THE ROMAN EMPIRE

Contents

SECTION TWO—THE 160 QUESTIONS INTERVIEWERS ASK AND HOW TO ANSWER THEM   117

SECTION THREE—ENHANCING YOUR INTERVIEWING SKILLS   141

SECTION FOUR—POST-INTERVIEW ACTIVITIES   159

Preface

This book was written to answer the five questions that people ask most often when they start looking for a job:

- How do I get the right kinds of interviews?
- What will interviewers ask me, and what are the best answers I can give them?
- Besides giving great answers, what else can I do at my interviews to make the best possible impression?
- When I want the job, what can I do after the interview is over?
- How do I make sure I'm offered the highest possible salary?

These questions reveal a key characteristic of job-seekers: They're apprehensive about the job-search process because they're not knowledgeable about all the steps to take. That's a natural way to feel, so if you have doubts about how to proceed and reservations about looking for a job, don't be concerned. After you've read this book, you'll have all the information you need and the self-assuredness you want.

Two factors heighten job-seekers' concern and sometimes cause them to call off their search prematurely; this happens no matter how much people want a certain position or how talented they are in their work.

First, there's the competition from other job-seekers. It's been estimated that during any given month over 13,000,000 Americans are in the job market, because they are unemployed, want to change companies, or want to make a complete career change. This stiff competition always brings rejection. And no one likes being rejected.

Second, job-hunting can be very frustrating when someone doesn't know the ropes. From the day a search is begun, people want to know what's going to happen next. They're always asking themselves, *Will I be given an interview? When will the interview take place? What did the interviewer think of me? When will the interviewer finish seeing all the other candidates? Will there be a second interview? When will the interviewer make his decision? When will I be told where I stand? When? When? When!*

Unfortunately, job-seekers must be patient and wait for prospective employers to give them answers. When people aren't skilled in looking for a job, that long-awaited reply often brings disappointment and frequently outright rejection.

Many job-seekers—just to escape this disheartening situation—give up their search and remain with their current employers. Others accept the first offer that comes their way, even though the job is less challenging and rewarding than the position they originally set out to find.

The information provided in this book will enable you to manage all the problems and difficult situations you'll encounter. Armed with this guide's advice and your newfound confidence, you'll know exactly what to do and when to do it every step along the way. You'll be in command of your job-search campaign, rise above the competition, and find the position of your choice in the shortest possible time.

In the pages that follow, there are many references to "the manager" and "the company."

Manager refers to the individual who has the authority to hire you. Depending on your level of seniority, this person could range from a staff member to the chief executive officer or owner.

Company pertains to any potential employer. This might be a business, an educational institution, a medical facility or practice, a law firm, a social services or charitable organization, or the government. The book's principles apply to seeking employment in all fields.

For the purpose of simplicity, this book is written in the masculine gender. It pertains, of course, to men and women equally.

SECTION ONE

"How do I get the right kinds of interviews?"

30 WAYS TO OBTAIN INTERVIEWS

Introduction

Like most job-seekers, you probably believe that the hardest part of job-hunting is getting the right interviews. The truth of the matter is that obtaining interviews is easier than you think. In fact, even as you read this paragraph, two fundamentals about the job market are at work in your behalf.

First, companies are always hiring new people.* This is to fill the steady flow of vacancies that arise from continuous promotions, transfers, terminations, resignations, retirement, and, most notably, the creation of new positions to achieve organizational growth.

Because companies have this ongoing need for personnel, interviews will automatically result if you contact the right individuals and present your qualifications in a convincing way. The job-search strategies described in this section will assure that you perform these key tasks successfully.

Second, the market is much larger than it appears. Most people consider "the market" to consist of the openings they can identify quickly. These are the positions that are advertised in newspapers and listed with employment agencies. Companies have limited recruiting budgets, however, and such jobs account for only about 20% of the vacancies that actually exist. The other 80% aren't made public. They are "hidden" but are just as real. The same strategies will produce interviews for these unknown openings as well as for the positions that are easy to detect.

---

* Although hiring activity varies with changes in economic conditions, there's always an abundance of job openings, even during recessionary times. This is the case right now, when Fortune 500 companies have been making front-page news with their announcements of massive layoffs, downsizings, and early-retirement programs. Throughout this difficult period, many people have been making successful job changes.

Thirty strategies are discussed in the pages that follow. They are grouped into five categories: networking, direct mail, telephone presentation, media advertisements, and registration.

As you become familiar with these different approaches, you'll decide which ones will work best for you. Your selections will depend on the following factors: your level of seniority, whether you're pursuing a career change or advancement in the same field, whether you're employed or unemployed, your need for confidentiality in looking for a job, whether you want to remain in the same locale or move to another part of the country, how quickly you must find a position, how much time you have available to work on your search and go on interviews, and how effectively you can communicate on the telephone.

By using the strategies that fit your situation and needs, you'll set up a maximum number of interviews, both for the position you want and with the kind of organization you want.

As a guide for selecting the best strategies to work with (never rely on one method alone), here are the approaches that will produce the most interviews, depending on your particular goals and circumstances. Although these strategies don't represent the complete list, they are the most reliable and should be considered first. (The numbers in the list refer to the numbered strategies of Section One.)

If You're Unemployed and Need Interviews Immediately

- Telephoning a Potential Employer
- Personal Contacts
- Employment Agencies (only when an agency specializes in your field)
- Telephoning Managers in Response to Advertisements
- Broadcast Letter (especially for contacting a large number of companies)

If You're Employed and Require Confidentiality

- Personal Contacts and Third-Party Correspondence (particularly for contacting companies in your own industry)
- Media Advertisements, nos. 17, 18, 19, 20
- Executive Search Firms
- Employment Agencies (only when an agency specializes in your field)
- Broadcast Letter (so long as your name isn't well known)

If You Want to Make a Career Change

- Personal Contacts
- Information Interviewing
- Third-Party Correspondence (through direct mail as well as answering ads)
- Professional Organizations and Trade Shows

If You're Seeking Advancement in the Same Field

- Personal Contacts
- Telephoning a Potential Employer
- Employment Agencies (only when an agency specializes in the field)
- Broadcast Letter
- Media Advertisements, nos. 17, 18
- Executive Search Firms

If You're a Junior-Level Job-Seeker

- College and Alumni Placement Offices
- Personal Contacts
- Information Interviewing
- Media Advertisements, no. 17
- Telephoning a Potential Employer

- Employment Agencies
- Broadcast Letter

If You're a Senior-Level Job-Seeker

- Personal Contacts
- Media Advertisements, nos. 17, 18
- Broadcast Letter
- Executive Search Firms

If You Wish to Relocate

- Broadcast Letter
- Personal Contacts
- Employment Agencies and Media Advertisements, no.
  17 (only when you have exceptional qualifications)

Before exploring these different strategies, a few words should be said in case you're unemployed:

You might think that you're at a disadvantage by being out of work. Not at all—especially during recessionary times. In fact, the Labor Department stated that during the slow economy of 1991, one in every five families had an unemployed member. Potential employers will certainly require a good explanation for why you're not working, but being unemployed is not a handicap.

And even if you were fired, being terminated by a company doesn't carry the stigma it used to. *Business Week* estimated that 500,000 managers are let go each year. The number of people dismissed from less senior positions exceeds this figure.

More important, there are actually two benefits to being unemployed:

First, you can devote 100% of your time to your job-search campaign, enabling you to take every conceivable step that might bring you closer to getting the offer you want. The employed job-seeker doesn't enjoy this luxury.

Second, you don't require confidentiality in looking for a job. This allows you to use any one of the 30 job-search strategies, plus exploit each method to the fullest extent possible. As a result, you'll gain greater exposure and obtain that many more interviews.

Instead of regretting the fact that you're unemployed and wishing it weren't the case, realize the opportunities it provides.

Networking

Networking has the same purpose in job-hunting as it does in any other activity: to meet new people through referrals made by mutual acquaintances. When looking for a job, you can use these referrals to gain an interview, to be introduced to someone who can arrange an interview for you, to get advice about your job search, or to obtain information about a new career you're considering.

In order to appreciate the value of networking as a job-search strategy, you must understand the power of a referral. It provides two key benefits: It dramatically increases the likelihood of getting both interviews and offers, and it has the potential to produce interviews under the most desirable of circumstances—you will have no competition from other job-seekers. These benefits will be explained in detail in the discussion that follows.

Here are the networking strategies:

1. Personal Contacts

Arranging interviews through personal contacts is the only strategy that's effective for all job-seekers, regardless of their level of seniority, objectives, or the circumstances under which they're conducting a search. It should therefore be the first strategy you consider using.

As stated above, approaching potential employers through personal contacts increases your chances of generating interviews as well as offers. There's a reason for this: You have immediate credibility.

When you're introduced to someone by a mutually respected

third party, you've been prescreened and aren't regarded as "one of the masses." Employers see you as a choice prospect and look for reasons why they should hire you instead of reasons why they should not. There isn't any of the skepticism that usually accompanies the interview situation.

In fact, no matter how impressive your resume and accomplishments might be, they won't mean as much to a prospective employer as the recommendation from an individual whose judgment he trusts. This recommendation will guarantee an interview when an opening exists. It will sometimes produce an interview even when there is no opening. And it will increase the likelihood of being selected for hire when you're one of several equally qualified candidates under consideration for a position. All this is borne out by the statistic that approximately 75% of company hirings are the result of employee referrals.

The second benefit of meeting potential employers through personal contacts is that you can have interviews without competition from other job-seekers. This situation can occur in three different ways:

1) When you meet potential employers through personal contacts, you automatically gain exposure to the positions that are not being advertised or listed with employment agencies. These are the 80% of the openings that actually exist—the hidden job market. With many of these positions, there will be no applicants under consideration. This is because the other job-hunters are focusing their efforts elsewhere, on the openings that they know about, the other 20% of the job market.

2) A manager is always interested in improving his department by hiring additional talent. Once he meets you, he can then decide to create a position for you. Here, there is no competition because the position did not even exist; the manager had no reason to be conducting interviews.

Further benefits also accrue from this situation. While being interviewed, you aren't evaluated against an existing job description or profile of "the ideal candidate." In addition, there are no predetermined limits on the scope of your responsibilities or your salary. The position is being created around your capability and is being tailored to meet your needs.

3) A manager often has future plans to hire additional staff members. If you have the type of background he'll be looking for, he may decide to move up his schedule and hire you at this time. It's advantageous for the manager to do so: Not only is he assured of finding the right individual, but he avoids the time-consuming task of conducting interviews and thus eliminates the steep recruiting costs that would come from his budget.

If your goal is to change careers—as it is for so many people these days—using personal contacts will be an especially effective way to develop interviews. Because you won't have the directly related experience that employers look for, an endorsement from a mutual acquaintance who can vouch for your capability becomes that much more important.

Now that you understand the value of a referral and the power of networking, let's discuss who your contacts can be and how to manage the networking process.

Your contacts can include a wide variety of people: fellow employees; former co-workers; business associates employed by customers, suppliers, and competitors; and fellow members of professional organizations and trade associations, as well as friends, family members, neighbors, club members, accountants, bankers, stockbrokers, insurance agents, lawyers, doctors, clergymen, civic and community leaders, and college and high school alumni. The possibilities are almost endless.

In order to network effectively, you must have a well-thought-out and highly organized plan for advising your contacts of your availability, the type of work you want to do, and your qualifications for this position. An integral part of this plan will also be to cultivate new contacts along the way. If all you do is tell a dozen or so people whom you already know that you're looking for a job and give each one a copy of your resume, you'll be leaving your success up to chance.

The best approach to take is what's known as the "targeted" approach. This is where you make a list of the companies with which you want interviews—either because of the industry or field they're in, their size, their location, or some other important factor—and then systematically go through the list. The first step, therefore, is to compile such a list of potential employers. Call it List A. If you need assistance in identifying companies to approach, many sources are available.

To identify companies by industry

Thomas Register, Standard Directory of Advertisers, Moody's Industrial Manual, Value Line Investment Survey, International Directory of Corporate Affiliations, Dun & Bradstreet's *Million Dollar Directory* and *Middle Market Directory* group 150,000 companies by product line and type of service rendered.* To make sure you haven't missed any organizations that are subsidiaries of companies, you might want to check the *Directory of Corporate Affiliations.* This publication cross-indexes subsidiary companies by type of business.

If you want to know which companies are the leaders in their industry, see *Ward's Business Directory.* It ranks 51,000 companies according to industry sales.

In addition, *Guide to American Directories for Compiling Mailing Lists* and *Principal Business Directories for Building Mailing Lists* state the industries that have directories of their own, including the names of the publications.

---

* These reference books, along with state directories, also list companies' sales volume and/or number of employees. This will help you select the size company you want.

Most of the above reference books can be found at your library.

Many professional and trade associations publish directories that list their member firms. *The Encyclopedia of Associations, The Encyclopedia of Business Information Sources,* and *National Trade and Professional Associations of the United States* contain the names and addresses of associations throughout the country. You can also call one or two of the largest companies in the industry in which you want to work and ask to be transferred to the president's secretary. This person will have the name and address of the association you need. Also, ask if there's a local chapter or an independent association that's in the immediate area.

To identify companies by geography

There may be a local or regional professional association for the companies in the industry you're interested in. Again, if you call the secretary to the president at one or two of the largest companies in the geographic area that interests you (the *Yellow Pages* will be helpful here), you'll be able to get contact information on the secretary or president of the local association, if one exists. This person may be able to provide you with a list of the members.

Moody's Industrial Manual, Million Dollar Directory, Middle Market Directory, Directory of Corporate Affiliations, Directory of Foreign Manufacturers in the United States, Directory of American Firms Operating in Foreign Countries, International Directory of Corporate Affiliations, and *Bottin International Business Register* cross-index companies geographically.

The Thomas Publishing Company puts out regional guides that provide the names of manufacturers of different products located in various geographic areas.

Each state publishes a directory of its largest employers. The companies are listed alphabetically, by city or town. (They are also cross-indexed by industry.)

The *Yellow Pages* groups companies by products and services within a limited geographic area. This source will be especially useful for finding small firms in the industry of your choice. The directory you need might be at the library. If not, you can purchase it from the regional telephone company.

A town's Chamber of Commerce will often have a list of the major employers in the area.

A final way to identify companies is to purchase a mailing list. Dun's Marketing Services and Standard & Poor's Corporation will compile a list of organizations according to your specifications for industry, location, and size (either in dollar volume or number of employees). Contact Dun's Marketing Services, Three Sylvan Way, Parsippany, NJ 07054 ([800] 624-5669), or Standard & Poor's Corporation, Dept. CDS, 25 Broadway, New York, NY 10004 ([212] 208-8300).

While compiling this list of potential employers, be on the lookout for companies that have announced impressive sales gains or have stated plans to build a new facility, expand an existing one, or offer a new product or service. These news items are usually the forerunners of increased hiring.

Once you know which companies will comprise List A, arrange them in the order of your preference. Then write down opposite each one the names of people you know, or know of, who might be able to set up an interview. (When you record the name of someone you *know of*, also write down the name of the individual who can introduce you to this person.)

Next, compile List B. This list will consist of the people you know or know of, who in general have a wide range of contacts and might be able to arrange appointments for you. These individuals could be business associates or personal friends and acquaintances. Don't put anyone on List B who's already on List A.

After you've completed both lists, you'll be ready to start the networking process by approaching your contacts. Begin with List A.

List A

Starting with the companies you're the most interested in, call each contact, explain that you're conducting a job search and the reason why, and tell the person that you're hoping he can arrange an interview for you with a certain company or set of companies. Then give the name(s) of the organization(s).

If you're on close terms with a contact, it will be advantageous to meet with this individual in person to show him the entire list. It's possible that he'll be able to arrange interviews for you at companies other than those that you were aware of. This meeting will also provide the opportunity for him to suggest other people for you to call, when there are companies you want to see but don't know anyone who can set up an appointment.

Always explain to your contacts that they don't have to introduce you to the manager of the department in which you want to work. This is the ideal situation, of course, but it will suffice if an initial appointment can be arranged for you to "get your foot in the door." Once you've met with someone at a company, you can then be introduced to the manager who can hire you.

If a contact tells you that he can't arrange an appointment, ask if he knows or knows of someone who can. This will enable you to expand your network of contacts. In addition, give your contacts a copy of your resume so they'll have a clear understanding of the position you're seeking and your qualifications for it. Having your resume on hand will also make it easier for them to set up interviews.

Utilizing List A this way has the potential to produce extremely quick results. In a matter of a week or so, you might be able to gain interviews with many choice companies. A factor that will influence your success, however, is how actively companies are hiring new people. If business conditions are strong, a large number of interviews may be arranged for you. If you're job-hunting during a recessionary period, though, and companies are contracting rather than expanding, you'll have less success. You might then have to use another approach—asking your contacts to refer you to people *for advice about your job search*, and not to be interviewed for a job. This alternate method will be discussed shortly.

An interview with a potential employer can be arranged in two different ways. A contact can set it up himself (the preferred method), or he can give you the name of the individual to see and allow you to arrange the meeting. In the latter case, you can either call this person on the phone or write a letter, which you will follow up with a phone call.

If you decide to write a letter, begin your correspondence by referring to your mutual acquaintance and his suggestion that the two of you meet. Next, explain that you're looking for a position and state the type you have in mind. Then summarize your experience, citing your accomplishments, responsibilities, educational background, and any other data that will enhance your qualifications. (For assistance in summarizing your background in letter form, follow the procedures for writing a broadcast letter, detailed in job-search strategy no. 4. However, so that your correspondence can begin as above, delete the broadcast letter's opening sentence and use the information contained in this sentence as the first item in your background summary. For an example of a broadcast letter, see page 35.) Conclude by stating that you will call in a few days to follow up.

Placing phone calls to potential employers, however, is usually more effective than writing letters, especially when contacting *local* companies. It's best to use this approach.

When calling someone, you'll often reach their secretary. Introduce yourself by giving the name of the individual who suggested that you call. Your call will be put through at once or returned shortly thereafter.

When you actually speak with the person you're calling, introduce yourself by giving the name of your mutual acquaintance. Then offer a one- or two-sentence overview of your background, being sure to mention an important accomplishment or responsibility. Conclude by stating that you're calling to see if a meeting can be set up to discuss a position at his company.

Before you begin making these calls, have notes to refer to. This will help you make a smooth presentation and assure that you don't omit any important information. Some job-seekers find it beneficial to first practice these calls, initially by themselves and then through role-playing with their spouse or a friend.

Because you have a referral, many people will agree to see you. However, there's no guarantee that an interview will be set up, and you might be asked to send in your resume. There are two ways to handle this request:

If your resume reveals negative points that might dissuade someone from wanting to meet you (examples are job-hopping and periods of unemployment), explain that you're revising the document but will immediately send a letter that outlines your background. (The discussion on the broadcast letter also explains how to present your experience without disclosing any liabilities.) Begin the letter by noting this phone call and the person who referred you. Conclude by stating that you'll be calling to follow up.

The other approach is to send a resume as requested. Always enclose a cover letter that refers to this call and your mutual acquaintance, and concludes by stating that you'll be telephoning to follow up.

Which method you use will depend on how favorably your resume sets forth your background, plus how much free time you have to write individually tailored letters.

Aside from being asked to send a resume, you may be told that an interview can't be arranged because there are no openings. In this instance there are two steps to take: First, ask for referrals to managers at other companies who might have openings. Then offer to send your resume for future reference. This will enable the individual to contact you if a position arises or if he hears of one at another company.

List B

Depending on how many interviews you've arranged through your contacts on List A, you might not even need to use List B. But if you do, here's how to proceed:

When you know someone extremely well, call him on the phone, explain your current situation, and set up a meeting to go over your list of potential employers. This person will undoubtedly be able to arrange interviews for you or introduce you to someone who can. Also ask if there are any other companies with which he could set up an appointment. Always give this contact an ample supply of resumes.

When you're less familiar with someone, call him on the phone, explain your situation and ask if you may send him your resume to see if he can arrange interviews for you. Also tell him that you've compiled a list of companies with which you would like interviews and ask if you may enclose the list. Conclude the conversation by stating that you'll call back in a few days to follow up.

During this subsequent conversation, you may decide to ask for referrals to other people for similar assistance. Whether or not you do will depend on how helpful this person is and how many interviews you have already arranged.

When deciding the order in which to approach people, call them according to their ability to help you, not according to how well you know them. Often your best referrals will come from people you know the least.

If there is someone whom you don't know well enough to call on the phone, but who could be extremely helpful, you can write a letter to this person instead of calling.

Ideally, asking personal contacts to arrange interviews for you will produce the meetings you need to get the offer you want. As already discussed, though, if business conditions are poor and companies aren't actively adding personnel, this approach might not be as successful as you would like. In this case you can work with your contacts in a slightly different manner.

Ask your contacts to arrange appointments for you for the purpose of *getting advice about which companies to see*, and not for a job interview. This will enable you to meet many more people than you would by trying to set up job interviews. First of all, people don't have to have a job opening in order to agree to meet you, and the likelihood is that at any given time there won't be a vacancy for someone with your background. Second, most people are willing to chat with someone as a favor to a friend.

When setting up these interviews, your contact will explain to the person he wants you to meet that you're looking for a job, but don't expect to be interviewed for an opening at his company. He will make it clear that your reason for meeting him is to get his advice on people to contact. His phone call could go something like this: "John, I recently spent some time talking with a fellow named Jack Bartello. Jack's very capable, and he's looking for a key marketing slot in industrial products, preferably chemicals. Would you meet with him for a few minutes? You might have some ideas of good people for him to contact."

Sometimes, though, a contact might ask *you* to set up this advice interview. Your success in arranging this meeting will often depend on how close a relationship your contact has with the person he suggests you see. (Always get this information in advance of your phone call.) If the two are on close terms, you probably won't have to do any more than mention the name of the individual who referred you and explain why you're calling.

However, if the relationship isn't a close one, you might have to be more persuasive during your call. An effective approach would be: "(First and last name of the person who referred you) suggested I call you. He told me about your years of experience in (name of his field or industry) and how knowledgeable you are about the companies and people in the industry. I'm looking for a new position, and since networking is the most effective way to set up interviews, I'm using it as the crux of my job search. (First name of the person who referred you) thought you might be able to help me by suggesting people for me to contact. Briefly, (describe your background and the type of position you're seeking). Can we arrange a time to get together?"

If you go on enough of these interviews for advice—including interviews for advice that are set up as a result of these initial interviews—you'll meet people who will make you offers. They'll either have an existing opening, create a position for you, or want to hire you at this time instead of an unknown person at a future date.

There are two important questions to ask during these advice interviews: "Do you know of any companies that are growing right now and that might be adding personnel?" and "A couple of my choice targets are _____. Do you know anyone who works at these companies?" (If this person seems eager to help you, then show him your complete list of target companies.) At the beginning of a meeting for advice, always give your new contact a copy of your resume so that he'll have a good understanding of the position you're seeking and your qualifications for it. Also, if he doesn't know anyone who will meet with you right now, ask if he can refer you to one or two people for getting this kind of advice.

When trying to set up interviews for advice, not everyone will agree to see you, of course. Some people will tell you that they're just too busy. When this happens, there are two approaches to take. You can say something like: "(First name of the person who referred you) told me that you're extremely busy and that your time is limited. Instead of trying to find a time during the business day, could we get together for ten or fifteen minutes after work, perhaps over a cup of coffee?" A second possibility is: "(First name of the person who referred you) told me that you're extremely busy and might not have time to see me. He also said that of all the people he suggested I call for advice, you were at the top of his list. Could I fax you my resume and call you back tomorrow? Perhaps you'll have some ideas of people for me to contact."

A further way to set up a meeting for advice—as well as to *start* a networking process in a specific field or industry—is to write a letter to an executive who holds a senior-level position at a company in the field or industry you're interested in. (See page 23 for the way to learn the names and titles of key company employees.) This approach will be especially helpful if you're just starting out in your career or have recently moved to a new part of the country (in these instances, job-hunters can't expect to have a wide circle of contacts to draw upon).

Begin your letter by giving a brief summary of your background. Be sure to include one outstanding accomplishment, responsibility, or set of strengths.

Then explain that you're writing this person because of the responsible position he holds at a company in the _____ industry (or field), that you're trying to arrange interviews with companies in this industry (or field), and that your hope is that he'll be able to suggest good organizations or people for you to contact.

Conclude your letter by stating that you'll call in a few days to see if a brief meeting can be arranged for this purpose.

When you place your follow-up call, you may reach a secretary who will ask why you're calling. Explain that you're following up on a letter you recently wrote to the person you wish to speak with. This will facilitate your call being put through. (For more information on telephoning people without a referral, see the discussion "Telephone Presentation," page 54.)

When using this approach, some individuals won't take your call. Others will tell you that they have no idea of people for you to contact. But then there will be those people who will be sympathetic to your situation and who will want to help you. They will agree to set up an appointment, and you will have successfully begun your networking process.

If you're ever tempted to try to save time by calling people on the phone instead of writing letters when contacting executives for advice without a referral—don't. Since you're asking someone you don't know to do you a favor, you'll have much more success if you go through the trouble of writing a letter. The person you're writing to will appreciate your effort and the length you've gone to; in turn, he'll be more inclined to help you.

Granted, going on interviews for advice will be time-consuming, and you'll probably have to meet with a large number of people before you're made an offer. But meeting many people is what networking is all about. In fact, there's a saying in the employment field: "Networking works if you work it." Meet as many people as you can—your perseverance will be rewarded.

Whether you should ask your contacts to arrange job interviews for you or introduce you to people for advice and additional referrals is a matter you need to decide at the outset of your job search. Discuss this with your closest contacts and get their opinions as to which approach would be more effective. If you find that you're having difficulty getting job interviews, however, asking your contacts to refer you to people for advice is clearly the next step. Needless to say, if you're able to arrange interviews for advice with people who also work at the companies you're interested in joining, you'll be covering two bases at the same time.

Another point to consider when getting interviews through personal contacts is your need for confidentiality. If you're unemployed or if confidentiality isn't important, you're free to approach as many people as you want and to generate as much exposure as you can. Clearly, the more people who are aware of your availability, the more openings that will be brought to your attention.

If you're employed and must maintain a low profile, you'll have to be selective about the individuals you approach. One of the outstanding features of generating interviews through personal contacts, though, is the enormous ground a contact can cover for you, especially if he's well known in your field. He can call managers, describe your background, and try to find openings for you or interest managers in creating a position *without reveal-*

ing your identity. Ask your contacts to make as many of these calls as possible.

Networking Tips

The following are important steps to take that will increase the success of your networking activities:

Whenever you're given referrals, always tell the person who gave you these introductions that you'll call him in a few weeks to apprise him of your progress. Not only is this courteous, but during your follow-up call you might be given the names of additional people to contact. Depending upon the amount of rapport you've established with this person, you might want to call again in a month or so to report on your progress. This continual follow-up activity will help you to keep your contact actively engaged in your job search.

The same day you initially met with someone, write a thank-you letter in which you express your appreciation for the referrals. Reiterate that you'll be calling in a few weeks to report on your progress. Also note on a calendar when to make this follow-up call.

Keep records of each meeting you have. Using 3" × 5" cards, write down the name of the person you saw (including his title and company), the date of the meeting, the name of the person who introduced you (if any), whether the meeting was for a job interview or for advice, any names of people you were given to call, important comments that will help you in future meetings, and planned follow-up activity including its date. This record keeping will be so helpful, in fact, that you should maintain notes on every interview you have, including interviews that result from the other job-search strategies.

When you have an especially good relationship with a contact, check in with him every two weeks or so throughout your job search. Don't be surprised if some people even ask you to do this.

2. Information Interviewing

If you're one of the many Americans who are thinking about making a career change, or are a graduating student looking for your first job, you may not be completely certain about the kind of work you want to do. It's likely that you have questions about the position or industry you're considering and want information on some important matters before you actually launch your job search.

Instead of just doing research at the library and speaking with close friends and family members to get their opinion about whether or not a position would be a good career choice, you will gain an advantage by talking to people who are engaged in this line of work. You will fulfill two missions at the same time: You will gain clarity on whether or not this would be a sound career move, and in the process of gathering this information and meeting with different people you may also get job offers. This process is known as *information interviewing*. Just as in meeting with people for advice, it too affords the opportunity to uncover an existing opening, to have a position created for you, and to be referred to people at other companies who might hire you.

Obtaining the Interview

When arranging information interviews, the person you want to meet with is the *manager who has the authority to hire you*. Make a list of the companies you might be interested in joining and obtain the name and title of this person at each one. There are different ways to get names and titles of managers:

Standard Directory of Advertisers; Million Dollar Directory; Middle Market Directory; Standard & Poor's Register of Corporations, Directors and Executives—Volume 1; and state directories provide names and titles of companies' key employees.

There can be a problem, however, with these directories. At the time you use them, some of the individuals listed may no longer be working at the company. Therefore call the companies to verify that your information is correct.

You can also call a company to find out the name and title of a manager who isn't mentioned in a directory. The person at the switchboard will usually know who heads up each department. If not, ask to be transferred to the appropriate department or functional area of the company. If you're still unable to obtain the name you want, ask for the name of the manager at the next level up. If necessary, go to the level of president. Job-seekers contact presidents all the time, especially when they hold senior positions or are approaching small companies.

When placing your call, never mention that it concerns employment. You'll invariably be transferred to the personnel department. This department is reluctant, and often forbidden by company policy, to disclose the names of employees.

If asked why you need an individual's name and title, explain that you want to write a letter to the person who oversees that department. It's unlikely that you'll be asked any further questions.

If you have a personal contact who can set up an interview, have this introduction made. If you don't know anyone who can refer you to a company, then approach the manager directly. The best way to do this is by writing him a letter.

Begin your correspondence by explaining that you're researching the manager's field because you're considering it for future employment. Next, request a 10-minute meeting for the purpose of gathering information. Then briefly summarize your background so that the manager will be familiar with your experience and the person who wants to meet him. Conclude by stating that you'll call in a few days to follow up.

When describing your background, *never* include accomplishments. If you do, you'll appear to be "selling" yourself and a manager will think you're really looking for a job interview and not for information.

When you place your follow-up call, you'll meet with the same resistance as discussed in job-search strategy no. 1 when contacting an executive for advice without having a referral: Secretaries will want to know why you're calling before they'll put your call through, and some managers won't give you any assistance at all. You'll also encounter two new situations:

Some managers will suggest answering your questions at this time or arranging a future phone conversation for this purpose. Make every effort to steer such a conversation toward when the two of you can meet in person. Otherwise, you'll get part of the information you want, but there won't be any opportunity to develop a relationship with the manager and to generate referrals and possible job offers. Often just stating that you feel a personal meeting would provide for better rapport and communication will prompt a manager to accommodate you.

There will also be managers who will agree to see you. They may be curious about your enthusiasm for their specialty; they may be flattered that you're seeking them out for the information you need; or they may have an appreciation for your situation and want to give you the assistance you're requesting.

At the beginning of your phone conversation with these managers, always make reference to your letter, explain that you're gathering information on their field because you're considering it for future employment—make it clear that you're not looking for a job at this time—and ask for a 10-minute meeting.

As suggested in job-search strategy no. 1, first practice these calls before placing them. Also have notes to refer to when you actually call companies.

Making the Interview a Success
When going on information interviews, you want to make as favorable an impression as possible on each manager you meet. There's no telling which company or manager you might ultimately want to work for. The way to achieve the best results is by

asking intelligent questions about the position you're considering and the industry or field it's in. Good questions to ask include:

> *How do most people enter the industry (field)? or*
> *How did you break into the industry (field)?*
> *The position I'm interested in is _____. How strong are my qualifications for it?*
> *What can I do to improve my qualifications?*
> *What kind of job am I qualified for that will lead to this position?*
> *For someone coming in at my level, what kind of career path can I expect?*
> *What are the characteristics of the people who are successful at this work? What are their strongest skills?*
> *What do most people find difficult about this work? Are there any particular obstacles that you think I might encounter?*
> *What are the long-term trends that are influencing the industry (field) right now? What effect are they having on the position I'm considering?*
> *How do you see the industry (field) changing in the next few years?*
> *Where do you think there will be the most growth?*
> *Are there any particular difficulties that the industry (field) is experiencing right now?*
> *What professional publications do you recommend that I read?*
> *What would a realistic first-year income be? What could I expect to be earning in 5 years? In 10 years?*

Since you're in a learning mode, you'll make an especially favorable impression on a manager if your questions demonstrate that you've become knowledgeable about his company, particularly its history, recent activities and successes, current problems, and future plans. At the very least, you should be aware of the company's products and/or services and know what its size is, in either dollar volume or number of employees. If the company is publicly owned, you should also know whether it's earning or losing money, how much, and the current trend. The different ways to obtain this information are explained in Section Three in the discussion, "Research the Company or Its Industry."

An information interview will usually begin with the manager asking what it is that you want to know. First, give him a copy of your resume so he'll have a complete picture of your background. Then explain your current situation and what it is you're trying to learn.

Also, feel free to take notes. You are actually the "interviewer" and the manager is the "interviewee."

As you engage the manager in conversation, your meeting will go in one of two directions. He'll give you the information you need and leave matters at that, or he'll take a more active interest in you because he sees you as someone he might like to hire.

The following are signs that you've struck a responsive chord in a manager and that he's considering you for employment: (1) he begins to probe your background and the reasons for your interest in his field; (2) he starts to take notes; (3) he describes a need in his department and it's one you could obviously fill; and (4) he begins to talk enthusiastically about his company and describes the advantages of working for it.

Most information interviews, however, won't take this turn. At a certain point, the manager will state that he has answered your questions and must now conclude the meeting. Thank him for his time and help, but ask if he can refer you to managers at two or three other companies. Explain that he's given you the information you came for, but that you would like to gain additional exposure and hear other perspectives on the field.

If the manager gives you names, ask if you may use his name when contacting these individuals. He'll most likely consent to this and you will now have referrals. If you prefer, it's appropriate to call these managers on the phone instead of writing them a letter, since you were referred to them by somebody you both know. When placing each call, state the name of the manager who suggested you call, explain your purpose, and set up a brief meeting.

After each information interview, write a short note thanking the manager for his time and help, whether you were given referrals or not.

Once you've completed your information interviewing, you should have a good idea of whether or not you want to pursue the position you've been investigating. In the process of gathering information, you may also have been made an offer you want to accept.

In the event that you've defined the type of work you want to do but have not received an offer, call the managers for whom you'd like to work and update them on your situation. Explain that you've completed your research, have determined the position you want to hold, and ask if an interview can be arranged for this kind of job.

If the manager doesn't have an opening to discuss with you, you now have many contacts in the field and can network for job interviews, instead of information interviews.

As stated earlier, information interviewing is the most appropriate for job-seekers who are pursuing entry-level positions or who want to make a career change, since it's customary to investigate a field before entering it.

This approach is seldom appropriate for individuals who hold senior-level positions, since expertise in a field is usually a prerequisite for hire. There are two instances, however, when senior-level job-seekers can benefit from information interviewing.

The first is when someone is changing *industries*, not *fields*. This is where he wants to do similar work, but for a company that offers different products or services. An example would be the manufacturing manager who wants to move from the television industry to the computer industry. Because his manufacturing knowledge might be transferable, it would be appropriate for him to gather information on how these two industries differ from a manufacturing standpoint.

The other exception is the job-seeker who has recently moved to a new part of the country or who is investigating the area before relocating. He will want to find out what's happening in his specialty in that locale. In the process of gathering this information, he may generate job offers.

If information interviewing is appropriate for your situation, it's important to understand that this method for meeting managers has been greatly misused and abused in the past. Many job-hunters have told managers that they wanted to meet with them to find out about work they were considering for future employment, but when they arrived at the interview it was obvious that they were really looking for a job. Their "doing research" was just a guise to set up a personal meeting. As a result, don't be surprised if some managers are suspicious—and even challenge you—when you tell them that you're looking only for information, especially if you're unemployed.

3. Professional Organizations and Trade Shows

Another way to begin a networking process—especially to develop contacts in a particular field or industry—is to join professional organizations and to attend trade shows.

Professional organizations hold meetings on a regular basis—some monthly—and will frequently allow you to attend a session as a guest. For information about these meetings, call companies in your locale and get the name and phone number of the local organization's president.

Attending trade shows will usually be more productive if you're planning to make a job change at a future time, since you won't be able to meet people until the next event takes place. The professional organizations's president will be able to give you information about these functions as well. Contacting this person also presents an outstanding opportunity to get advice about companies to see (see job-search strategy no. 1).

When going to professional meetings, you'll find it easy to meet people and strike up conversations. Many organizations, in fact, schedule time for this networking activity before a meeting begins. To remember the different people you'll meet, plan to note on a sheet of paper, or on the backs of business cards you'll be given, something that makes an impression on you. It could be what someone looks like, a statement the person makes, a question he asks, or a topic the two of you discuss.

If you're employed, always bring with you an ample supply of business cards. If you're unemployed, bring several copies of your resume. Be judicious, however, about how many copies of your background you hand out. You don't want to appear desperate. You can always call someone on the phone the following day to continue your networking effort.

In the event that you've just moved to a new part of the country, contacting the president of a professional organization will be an excellent way to begin your job search by launching a networking process.

Clearly, the cornerstone of networking is the development of referrals. Your pursuit of these introductions, however, shouldn't be limited to the networking strategies.

Consider anybody you speak with, regardless of the strategy that initiated contact, as a source for referrals to other companies. For example, if you're told that your background isn't appropriate for an organization's needs, ask for introductions elsewhere. Or, if a manager sends you a letter informing you that he won't be extending an offer, call to thank him for advising you and then ask if he knows of openings for you at other companies.

The suggestions from these managers are especially valuable. Since they have interviewed you, they understand your abilities and personality. They can judge accurately where you will fit in at other organizations.

Unfortunately, few job-seekers take these additional steps. This costs them an immeasurable number of interviews and offers.

Direct Mail

Direct mail is developing interviews by sending companies a letter that outlines your background.

In order for direct mail to be effective, you must write to the manager who has the authority to hire you, addressing him by name and title. (Job-search strategy no. 10 is an exception.)

Don't write to the personnel department. This is not to undermine the importance of this department; it plays a vital role in the successful functioning of an organization. When it comes to hiring, however, the final decision is almost always made by an applicant's prospective manager. As in any other endeavor, it's advantageous to deal directly with the ultimate decision-maker.

4. The Broadcast Letter

Of the 30 job-search strategies, sending companies a broadcast letter gives you the most exposure in the quickest manner.

The broadcast letter also provides four key advantages: First, it affords the opportunity to develop an interview with any company of your choice. Second, it enables you quickly and efficiently to contact any number of potential employers. Third, it allows you to tailor your background to fit the requirements of the position you're seeking. Fourth, it enables you to present only the information that will interest a company in hiring you. You can omit all information on which you might be screened out.

The broadcast letter should therefore be one of the first strategies you consider when you don't have personal contacts to arrange interviews with companies you're interested in. Although this letter lacks the credibility that a personal referral provides, it compensates for this by the speed with which it enables you to put your background and qualifications in front of any number of potential employers.

Even if you don't decide to use this method for generating interviews, you should still be knowledgeable about how it works. The broadcast letter is the cornerstone for presenting experience in letter form, and some of the strategies you'll want to utilize will require a written summary of your background. (Furnishing a resume will be less effective. This will be explained shortly.)

To demonstrate the broadcast letter approach, the background of Jack Bartello will be used:

Like most job-seekers, Jack's work history consists of negative as well as positive points. Jack has job-hopped, he must account for two periods of unemployment, and his objective is to join a large company that manufactures industrial products, preferably chemicals. Although his choice is to be a sales manager, he will consider positions as sales training manager and key account sales representative.

Examples of Jack Bartello's resume and broadcast letter are given on the following pages.

Jack P. Bartello
115 Navarre St.
Hyde Park, MA 02136
(617) 361-0576

OBJECTIVE   Sales Manager, Sales Training Manager, or Key Account Sales Representative for a large company manufacturing chemicals or industrial products.

EDUCATION   B.S., Chemistry, Rollins College, 1987.

EXPERIENCE   ALEXA CHEMICALS CO., Boston, MA. 1991–1993.
Regional Sales Manager for this manufacturer of industrial chemicals. Complete responsibility for sales to distributors in the 6 New England states.
- Increased sales 75% and brought the region from #7 in the country to #2 during this 2-year period.
- Terminated existing distributors and appointed new ones.
- Created sales training/motivation programs and trained distributors' sales personnel; these programs were adopted by Alexa Chemicals on a national basis.
- Exceeded quota each month.

ERVING REAL ESTATE, St. Louis, MO. 1990–1991.

MALONE CHEMICALS, INC., Philadelphia, PA. 1989–1990.
District Sales Representative for this distributor of industrial solvents. Sold to Fortune 500 companies, small businesses, colleges and universities, and municipalities, from the levels of executive to purchasing.
- Increased sales 50% in 1½ years.
- Increased dollar volume with existing customers and performed extensive prospecting to bring in new customers.
- Developed several new customers to National Key Account status.
- Trained new hires who were quickly promoted to district sales responsibilities.
- Exceeded quota each quarter.
Previously, Inside Salesman. Initial position was as Sales Administrator.

FAUCET CONSTRUCTION CO., Orlando, FL. 1988–1989.

COMMUNITY   Big Brothers of America, The United Way.
ACTIVITIES

PERSONAL   Married with 2 children, excellent health.

References furnished on request.

Jack P. Bartello
115 Navarre St.
Hyde Park, MA 02136
(617) 361-0576

①

December 20, 1993

② Mr. John F. Geer
National Sales Manager
Claude/Louie Polymer Co.
100 Summer St.
Boston, MA 01354

Dear Mr. Geer:

③ As Regional Sales Manager for a manufacturer of industrial chemicals, I increased sales 75% and brought my region from #7 in the country to #2 within a 2-year period. If you have a need for an individual with my capability, perhaps you would be interested in learning about my background. I ④ have:

⑤
- — increased sales by bringing in new customers, increasing dollar volume with existing customers, and changing distributors.
- — brought in new customers that I developed to National Key Account status in less than 1 year's time.
- — created unique sales training/motivation programs that were adopted by my employer on a national basis.
- — trained new hires who were quickly promoted to district sales responsibilities.
- — increased sales 50% within $1\frac{1}{2}$ years, while selling for a distributor of industrial solvents.
- — exceeded quota every sales period with an employer.

⑥ My account call includes Fortune 500 companies, small businesses, colleges and universities, and municipalities. I have sold to all levels of management, from executive to purchasing.

⑦ I have a B.S. in chemistry and am married with a family. Personal qualities include resourcefulness, excellent communication skills, a high level of motivation, plus the ability to motivate others.

⑧ I would be pleased to discuss the details of my qualifications during a personal interview.

Very truly yours,

Jack P. Bartello

Analysis of the Broadcast Letter and How to Compose It

1) Prepare your correspondence on personal letterhead. Omit a business phone number.

2) Write to the manager who has the authority to hire you, using his name and title. Since Jack was at the regional level, he contacted a manager at the national level.

In the event that your background is so strong that you think a manager might view you as a competitive threat and not interview you, contact the manager at the next level up. In this instance, Jack would write to the vice-president of sales.

3) The purpose of the opening sentence is to arouse a manager's interest so that he will read the letter in its entirety. (This is achieved in job-search strategy no. 1 by stating that a mutual acquaintance suggested that you write the letter.) Accordingly, cite your most *significant accomplishment* or *responsibility* (preferably the former) in regard to the position you're seeking. The accomplishment, however, need not have been with your current or most recent employer. Also, this sentence must never imply that you're unemployed or that the achievement wasn't a recent one. For this reason, don't begin with, "When I was a (your title), I (accomplishment)," or, "Two years ago, when I was a (your title), I (accomplishment)." Notice how Jack began, even though he was unemployed: "As Regional Sales Manager. . . "*

---

* Had Jack been currently employed, he would have written, "As Regional Sales Manager for a manufacturer of industrial chemicals, I have increased sales. . . ." Stating "I *have* increased sales" versus "I increased sales" is an even stronger implication of being currently employed.

When you describe the accomplishment, show its magnitude by using numbers. For example, instead of saying, "I significantly increased sales," write, "I increased sales 75%. . . within a 2-year period of time," as Jack did. In addition, use actual numbers, not words. Numbers have more impact. They also stand out and catch a reader's eye. Jack wrote "75%," not "seventy-five percent" and "2-year," not "two-year."

When you describe the company with which the accomplishment occurred, your wording should be such that the company resembles the kind of organization for which you want to work. Don't be so specific, however, that other types of companies might decline to interview you. Notice that Jack described his employer as a manufacturer of "industrial chemicals." Had he deleted "industrial" and just written "chemicals," he would have been less attractive to companies that were not in the chemical business. His wording allows all suppliers of industrial-type products to decide to interview him.

4) This sentence has two purposes. First, it indicates your interest in arranging an interview. Second, it implies the type of position you have in mind.

This sentence should never suggest that you're interested in one particular position (unless this is the case). You don't want to limit the kinds of jobs for which you can be considered.

Notice that when Jack referred to the type of person a manager might be looking for, he wrote "an individual with my capability." Once a manager reads the letter, he would see that Jack was qualified for several positions: sales manager, sales training manager, and sales representative. He could interview Jack for any of these.

Had Jack written "a sales manager," "a sales training manager," or "a key account sales representative," a manager would assume that this was the only responsibility in which Jack was interested. Jack would have precluded his being considered for other opportunities.

5) This section states additional accomplishments. List them in the order of their importance to the position you're seeking. Notice that Jack put his accomplishment as a district sales representative toward the end of the section. He also omitted the fact that he had performed extensive prospecting. Since his preference was to be a sales manager, he wanted to play down his experience as a sales representative.

Again, when describing the companies with which your achievements occurred, try to portray the companies as the kinds of organizations for which you want to work. Jack specified "industrial."

So that this section will stand out and catch a reader's eye, indent the sentences and precede each accomplishment with a dash. Also, begin each achievement with an "action" word. Jack selected "increased," "brought in," "created," "trained," and "exceeded." (See page 97 for a list of "action" words.)

If your background consists of administrative or support-type positions that don't lend themselves to visible accomplishments, list your major *responsibilities*. Wherever possible, use numbers to convey their scope. For example, state how many people or forms you processed each day, the dollar volume of the project you worked on, or the size of the facility, department, or company you worked at.

6) This section includes any additional information that will enhance your work history. Although Jack chose to describe the

breadth of his sales experience, the following are appropriate when they pertain to the type of job you want to hold: awards, honors, commendations, certifications, licenses, patents, inventions, copyrights, publications, foreign language proficiency, memberships in professional organizations or trade associations, community activities, hobbies, and military experience.

7) This section presents educational and/or personal information. If you don't have a college degree, omit educational information altogether. If you attended a college that isn't widely known or respected (as Jack did), delete its name. If you have a degree but your major is unrelated to your field, just state "B.S." or "B.A." If you'll be receiving a degree in the immediate future or are currently studying for an advanced degree, include this information. Never state that you're divorced, separated, or single (unless being single is advantageous for the position you're seeking).

8) This sentence reinforces your interest in an interview. Alternatives to what Jack wrote include: "I would be pleased to meet with you for a personal interview," "If you would like to meet me in person, please contact me at your earliest convenience," "If you would like to explore my qualifications further, I would be pleased to meet with you for a personal interview," and "If you would like to interview me, please contact me at your earliest convenience."

Notice that each piece of information Jack provided supported his qualifications to be a sales manager, sales training manager, or key account sales representative for a large company that manufactures industrial products, especially chemicals. Jack offered enough information about his chemical background to attract companies in the chemical industry. However, he didn't emphasize his chemical experience to the degree that companies in other industries would not be interested in him because they considered him to be too specialized for their businesses. His letter was consistent with his objective.

Also notice that Jack *omitted* certain data: his income level, age, number of years of experience, names of employers, company size, dates of employment, the year in which he was graduated from college, and the college he attended.

A broadcast letter almost always omits these items. Many managers have preferences regarding the types of people they hire, and this is the kind of data on which you can be screened out, even though you have the required technical experience. For example, a manager might feel that you have been earning too much or too little money. He could consider you to be too young or too old, or to have too much or not enough experience. He might not respect the companies you have worked for or the college you attended. He might not like to hire people from large companies or from small ones. He could see you as a job-hopper, or believe that because you've worked for one organization for so many years it would be difficult to adjust to another. He might question periods of unemployment or the fact that you currently aren't working.

To prevent being denied interviews for any of these reasons, omit this kind of information. Only provide data that will demonstrate your qualifications. No one can argue with accomplishments and success! If a manager is interested in the details of your background, he can find out about them by *interviewing you.*

Granted, once a manager meets you, he will learn about these details. However, you may not fit his stereotyped image and you won't be precluded from getting an offer. If a manager had this information in advance, he might never have arranged the interview.

If there's an aspect of your background you believe all managers will regard favorably, include it. For example, if you attended a highly respected college, state its name. If you have worked for prestigious companies, give their names.

If you're interested in a specific position or want to work in a particular industry, offer the kind of information that will enhance your qualifications for this objective. Likewise, if there's an aspect of your background that might be regarded unfavorably, omit it. Notice that Jack didn't write anything about the size of his employers or his sales volume. Since all his employers were small companies and his objective was to join a large organization, he didn't want to offer any information that might diminish the impact of his accomplishments. For example, he stated that he increased sales by 75%, not by $750,000. The latter wouldn't have been that impressive to an international chemicals company with annual sales in the billions of dollars.

In the event that you're an executive with an entrepreneurial bent and would like to join a company and put it into a new business, add a paragraph in which you suggest such a venture. While your accomplishments might prompt a reader to consider this himself, making the actual proposal will never hurt. Furnish a brief plan in which you cite the required capital, equipment, and personnel, plus projections for revenues and profits.

When composing the broadcast letter, try to keep the length to one page, although two are permissible. Also, don't attempt to write the letter in one sitting. You'll do the best work if you compose the document over a period of days. The letter won't sound the same to you in the morning as it did the night before. Always check for spelling, grammar, and punctuation.

At this point, you're undoubtedly wondering why you should go to the trouble of writing this letter and not just send companies your resume. Doing so would be a mistake. A broadcast letter will always produce more interviews. There are several reasons why.

Most important, a broadcast letter *will be read* by the manager to whom you send it. This is less frequently the case with a resume.

Many managers ask their secretaries to screen their mail and automatically route resumes to the personnel department. Since reading these documents is a time-consuming task, they prefer that a personnel representative conduct the initial evaluation.

Your broadcast letter won't be sent to personnel. Because you will mark the envelope "Personal & Confidential," most secretaries won't open it. They'll promptly give it to their boss. In the event that a manager has asked his secretary to open personal mail, he will still receive your correspondence. It's a letter and not a resume. There's no reason to send it to personnel.

When the manager sees your letter, he won't forward it to personnel either. First of all, virtually everyone reads mail marked "Personal & Confidential." Second, your opening sentence states an outstanding accomplishment in the manager's field. This arouses his curiosity and prompts him to read on. Third, your accomplishments in section 5 stand out because of the letter's layout; a manager can't help but read them.

There are other reasons why a broadcast letter is more successful than a resume:

You can't be screened out

When a manager has an opening for which you have the right experience, you can't be denied interviews because of hiring preferences. As already explained, a broadcast letter doesn't contain the kind of information that allows this to happen; a resume does. If you were to omit these items from your resume, their absence would be conspicuous. A manager could become suspicious that you were trying to conceal something unfavorable about your background and reject you.

Since your broadcast letter is a personal document, you have the freedom to say and/or leave out anything you want without ever arousing suspicion. You aren't bound by any traditionally followed practices, as you are in resume-writing, where certain information is always included.

If you compare Jack's letter to his resume, you'll see that it gives a manager every reason to interview him, but no reason to screen him out. His resume reveals several negative points: (1) he is unemployed; (2) he lacks in-depth experience as a sales manager; (3) he has job-hopped; (4) he has had a succession of positions in unrelated industries; and (5) he experienced a long period of unemployment after graduation from college. The resume depicts Jack as being extremely capable, but unstable and a high-risk candidate for long-term employment.

You can be interviewed for multiple positions

Since a broadcast letter doesn't state a formal job objective, a manager can interview you for any position for which you're qualified. A resume doesn't afford this luxury. No matter how skillfully you word your objective, you can still lose out on interviews. (If you omit an objective from your resume, many readers will assume that you have no career direction and are after any job you can get.)

In Jack's resume, although his objective reflects his priorities, it precludes his being considered for any positions that aren't directly related to outside sales. Had he included other possibilities, his objective would have stated too many job targets.

Not only will a broadcast letter produce more interviews than a resume, but these meetings can occur with no competition from other job-seekers. Just as with job-search strategy no. 1, you'll penetrate the hidden job market and gain access to the 80% of the openings that aren't being actively pursued by other job-hunters. In addition, you'll contact managers who will want to meet you with the objective of creating a position for you or hiring you today instead of hiring someone else with your background at a future time.

Compiling the Mailing List

Once you've composed your broadcast letter, the next step is to compile a mailing list. This will consist of the names and addresses of the companies you want to contact and the names and titles of the managers who could hire you. Use the sources listed on pages 11, 12, 13, and 23–24.

If you discover two or three potential managers at the same company, it's acceptable to send a letter to each one. Any individual who learns of your multiple letters will understand your keen interest in interviewing with his company.

How to Determine the Number of Companies to Contact

A broadcast letter usually generates interviews at a rate of 2% to 10%. For every 50 letters you send out, you can expect to set up from one to five appointments. (Sometimes you'll be asked to provide additional information before an actual time and date will be scheduled.)

If this percentage seems like a low return on your effort, you must take into consideration the number of interviews you can develop in so short a period of time, and that each one is with a company of your choice. No other strategy can produce these results.

Certain factors will affect the response rate of your letters and therefore the number of companies you need to contact. (These factors will influence the success of the other 29 job-search strategies as well.)

Economic and business conditions

The stronger the economy, the more actively companies hire new personnel. This will increase the success rate of the letter. The weaker the economy, the less the hiring activity. This will decrease the rate. The condition of the industries you're approaching will also play a part. At any given time, certain ones are prospering while others are experiencing adversity.

Your level of seniority

From a manpower standpoint, a company resembles a pyramid. There's less room at the top than at the bottom. The higher your level of seniority, the fewer the appropriate positions. For example, a company has only one president, while it employs many administrators. Senior-level job-hunters must therefore contact many more companies.

Company size

As a general rule, the larger the organization, the greater the number of people it can employ at your level. This increases the likelihood of openings. During the current recession of the early 1990s, however, the opposite has been the case. Large companies have been experiencing widespread downsizing and small companies have been growing and adding personnel. As a result, as this book goes to press, it's recommended that you contact a greater number of companies, and it will be to your advantage to approach as many small firms as possible.

Location

The farther you live from a company, the fewer your chances of generating an interview. Not only will a company find it expensive to meet you, but it will incur an additional relocation expense if it hires you. These costs decrease in importance, however, the higher the level of seniority.

The extent to which your skills are in demand

At any given time, certain types of experience are more sought-after than others.

The strength of your qualifications for the position you're seeking

Clearly, the stronger your skills, the easier it will be to get interviews.

As a guideline, contact between 50 and 100 companies. If necessary, write to as many as 500 or 1,000. In the latter case, it's suggested that you send an initial mailing to the 100 or 200 organizations in which you're the most interested. Additional mailings can be undertaken as needed.

If you'll be sending out only a few letters—to local companies—conclude your correspondence as follows: "I will call you in a few days to follow up." This call will increase the number of interviews. It will also provide the opportunity to develop leads and referrals.

When a manager wants to interview you, he'll usually contact you within one week of receiving your letter.

You'll also receive many replies from managers thanking you for contacting them, but explaining that there are no openings. Don't be discouraged by these "rejection" letters. Consider them as acknowledgment that your correspondence is being read. Then focus your attention on the companies that want to meet you. This is your audience of potential employers.

How to Prepare a Broadcast Letter for Mailing

If you don't have a word processor with a letter-quality printer (or have access to one), take your broadcast letter to a secretarial service. Also order stationery and envelopes.

Stationery should be 8½" × 11", of good quality, and contain your letterhead with zip code and telephone number. Recommended colors are ivory, light beige, and light gray. Have your return address printed on the back of the envelope.

Postdate the letter to allow sufficient time for printing, word processing, proofreading, making corrections, signing your name, collating, and putting on postage.

There are instructions to give the secretarial service concerning the preparation of the letter:

It must not be right-margin-justified. (This is when the type is spaced so that the letters line up evenly at the right margin.) You want the letter to look as if you typed it yourself, not like a document that was prepared by computer for mass mailing.

"Bullets" shouldn't be inserted where you use dashes. Only a computer-based keyboard has this character.

A secretary's initials shouldn't be typed in the lower left-hand corner of the letter. This suggestion might be made to give "a professional appearance" to your correspondence. Again, you want the letter to look as though you typed it yourself.

A secretary's initials could also lead prospective employers to believe that you were just terminated and your employer is providing you with secretarial assistance in looking for a job. Today many companies offer this service, especially to senior- and executive-level personnel. If you were just let go, you certainly don't want to "broadcast" this fact.

Have "Personal & Confidential" typed (not offset printed) in the lower left-hand corner of the envelope. The importance of this has already been explained.

When the letters are ready to be signed, do so in a pen with dark blue or black ink. Also, put the stamp on by hand. Machine postage conveys mass mailing.

How to Increase Your Number of Interviews

Within two weeks of mailing the letters, you will have heard from all the managers who want to interview you. If you want additional appointments, send a broadcast letter to the companies that weren't included in the initial mailing. Since you'll now have the results of the first mailing, you'll be able to gauge the number of companies to contact.

Another step that will add interviews is to call the managers from whom you haven't received a reply. This call will also provide the opportunity to develop leads and referrals, when managers have no openings to discuss with you.

If the initial mailing exhausted the list of potential employers, call the managers who sent you rejection letters. Thank them for answering your correspondence, then ask for suggestions concerning other companies to contact.

The importance of making these follow-up calls cannot be emphasized enough. You'll automatically increase your number of interviews by just calling each manager you wrote to.

Drawbacks to the Broadcast Letter

The broadcast letter is not without problems. Its biggest drawback is cost. In fact, it's the most expensive of the 30 job-search strategies. Although price decreases with volume, each letter can cost as much as $1.00. This expense is offset, however, by the speed with which the letter produces interviews and offers. If you're unemployed, it's costing you money every day you're not working. If you're employed, you're losing money each day you remain with your current employer, since you can expect to receive an increase upon changing jobs.

A second disadvantage is that the letter precludes confidentiality if you're well known in your industry or geographic area. Your interest in changing companies will undoubtedly leak back to your employer. For this reason, this strategy is often more suited to job-seekers who are unemployed, who are writing to companies in a different industry than their own, or who are contacting companies in another part of the country.

A third problem with the broadcast letter is that it's usually restricted to people who are seeking advancement in their field. If you're interested in changing careers, your accomplishments probably won't relate to the position you're pursuing. The letter will be of no use. You'll be better off trying to get interviews through the networking strategies.

A final problem is that this letter has been increasing in usage in recent years and some employers have come to view it more as a vehicle for concealing shortcomings than as a document for conveying qualifications. As a result, some employers are skeptical of individuals who use the broadcast letter approach.

Therefore, if you are fortunate enough to have excellent qualifications for the position you're seeking—with no factors in your work history that might preclude your being interviewed—consider sending companies your resume. This is particularly the case if you're unemployed (you don't need confidentiality) and you're pursuing a senior-level responsibility. In the latter case, employers often like to have a great many facts and details about an applicant before setting up a meeting.

The following are the other seven direct mail strategies; six of them incorporate a broadcast letter or variation of it.

5. Third-Party Correspondence

This strategy consists of having someone who is well known and respected in your field or geographic area write a letter of introduction for you to managers at different companies.

The letter presents your experience, significant accomplishments, and personal attributes, but *doesn't disclose your identity.* It also tells why the writer feels you're qualified for a certain position, states why you would make an outstanding contribution, and mentions that the writer will put the manager in touch with you to arrange an interview. This strategy enables you to "broadcast" your background while maintaining confidentiality as to your identity.

There's another advantage to this strategy: Many managers will want to meet you due to the outstanding recommendation from the influential person who's acting as your sponsor. It's therefore an excellent vehicle if you want to make a *career change.* The letter will give you credibility and generate interviews, even though you lack the experience a position traditionally requires.

If you have the appropriate individual to send this letter, "third-party correspondence" will produce more interviews than a broadcast letter.

The drawbacks to this strategy are: (1) you need the proper contact for writing the letter*, and (2) this person's reputation will probably be limited to a specific industry or geographic area.

---

* You can maintain anonymity by having a friend write this letter, but the fact that his name is unknown will result in far fewer interviews. If you try this approach, make sure your friend states that no fee is involved if the company interviews you or hires you. (It's possible that you could be denied interviews because someone believes you are actually being represented by an employment agency, which will charge a fee if you're hired.)

If you're currently employed, this strategy becomes more useful the higher your level of seniority. Since the likelihood increases that your name will be recognized, anonymity is needed with direct mail. "Third-party correspondence" provides this feature.

6. Writing to Managers Who Have Recently Been Promoted or Who Have Moved to a New Company

After managers have received promotions and, especially, joined new companies, they frequently want to build new staffs of their own. They are candidates for a broadcast letter.

To identify these individuals, read the *Wall Street Journal*'s daily column, "Who's News." It describes promotions and job changes occurring throughout the country. Also read the business section of the newspaper that serves the geographic area in which you want to work. The Sunday edition will be particularly helpful. It will usually include a column that lists promotions and job changes taking place in that region. In addition, read the trade publications for the industries and fields in which you're interested. They too announce promotions and job changes.

Because managers often require some time before they're ready to make staff changes, read back issues of these publications for up to eight weeks preceding the time you begin your search.

A potential advantage of this strategy is that you could contact a manager who's ready to hire someone but hasn't begun to conduct interviews. Here, you will face no competition from other job-seekers.

The disadvantage is that only occasionally will you read about a promotion that's appropriate for the type of position you're seeking.

7. Writing to the Previous Managers of People Who Have Recently Changed Companies

When someone has recently left a company, his replacement may not yet have been found. This could mean an opening for you. Send your broadcast letter to the manager to whom this person reported.

To obtain the manager's name and title, call the company and ask to be transferred to the appropriate department. Whoever answers the phone will have the information you want.

When a company is located out of town and you want to save the cost of this call, use the research publications at the library. (You can also call the reference librarian on the phone and ask for the name and title of the person you need. Advise which directories to use.)

As in the previous strategy, this job change information can be found in the *Wall Street Journal*'s "Who's News," the business section of newspapers, and trade publications. Again, read these publications for up to eight weeks preceding the time you begin your search.

The primary limitation of this strategy is that it's usually restricted to job-seekers who are at the level of manager and above. Most personnel changes that are published are at senior levels. In addition, only occasionally will you read about a job change that pertains to the position you're pursuing.

8. The Telegram

This approach is bold and dramatic. It consists of sending a manager a telegram that describes two or three of your outstanding accomplishments and states that your resume follows.*

---

* An alternate, even bolder approach is to conclude the telegram by stating that you will be calling the next day to discuss scheduling an interview.

This strategy can be effective when you know that a manager is currently conducting interviews. Its drama attracts his attention and assures that your resume will be read.

When using this approach, your aggressiveness must be supported by impeccable qualifications. In addition, the strategy is recommended only for positions that require an aggressive personality.

9. Contacting "Growth" Companies

Some job-seekers are especially interested in joining young, rapidly growing companies where potentially lucrative stock options are part of the compensation plan. These firms are excellent targets for a broadcast letter since their growth necessitates the continuous hiring of personnel.

To identify these kinds of companies, read *Financial World*'s annual directory on growth firms, *Business Periodicals Index*, which, under "Growth Firms," lists the magazines (including their dates) that contain articles on such organizations, and *Inc.* magazine's annual issue on the country's 100 fastest growing publicly owned companies.

10. Contacting Venture Capital Firms

Another way to reach young, rapidly growing companies, as well as companies that are in a "turnaround" state and are expecting a significant increase in business, is to send a broadcast letter to venture capital firms. The principals at these companies have a wide range of contacts within specific industries and are often aware of high-level openings. Because of their vested interests, they'll apprise their management teams of talent that has recently come into the job market.

To obtain the names and addresses of venture capital companies throughout the United States, you can purchase a copy of

National Venture Capital Association—Annual Membership Directory from the National Venture Capital Association, 1655 N. Fort Myer Drive, Suite 700, Arlington, VA 22209 ([202] 528-4370).

11. Providing a Post Office Box Number for Response

Another direct mail strategy that will maintain confidentiality is to send managers a broadcast letter that contains a post office box number for response.

This approach can be useful for contacting managers at competitors or at other companies in your industry or field. The letter is unsigned and provides no information that could reveal your identity. It conveys your expertise, however, and states that it's because you're in the same industry or field that you must initially remain anonymous.

Many managers will consider this approach "unprofessional" and won't answer your correspondence. Others will be so curious as to your identity that they'll contact you even though they have no openings to discuss. However, some managers will understand your need for confidentiality and will write back wanting to explore bona fide employment opportunities.

This isn't a preferred strategy, but it occasionally brings results. The higher a job-seeker's level of seniority, the less effective it becomes.

Telephone Presentation

Telephone presentation is trying to set up interviews by calling managers on the phone and describing your background.

These approaches require self-confidence and sound verbal skills. If you possess these qualities, this group of strategies will enable you to set up immediate interviews, as well as generate leads and referrals.

Telephone presentation also presents two problems:

The first is that calling managers on the phone becomes less effective as positions increase in seniority. A written summary of an applicant's background is usually required before an interview will be arranged. This is always the case when a company is located out of town.

The second difficulty is that these calls require privacy. Even if you have your own office, calling from work can be awkward. For this reason, this approach will be easier to implement if you're unemployed.

12. Telephoning a Potential Employer

The distinguishing feature of this strategy is the speed with which you can contact a select number of companies. The approach is especially effective when you know there's an opening for someone with your background.

To implement the strategy, make a list of the companies with which you want interviews. Next, obtain the names and titles of the hiring managers. Then systematically go through the list.

When placing these calls, you may encounter a problem getting past a secretary, since many managers have their calls screened. To avoid secretaries, try phoning before 8:30 A.M. or after 5:00 P.M. At these times, secretaries are often not at work and managers are in their offices preparing for or concluding the day's business. In addition, don't make these calls on Monday morning or on Friday afternoon. Many people are extremely busy at the beginning of the week and are looking forward to matters other than business at the end of it.

If you happen to reach a secretary, speak with confidence and authority and give both your first and last names. For example: "Good morning. Jack Bartello calling for Mr. Geer. Is he there, please?" If asked which company you represent, say, "Myself." If asked the nature of your call, say, "It's personal." Don't give the actual reason you're calling. If a secretary tells you that the manager is unavailable, ask when he'll be free and call back at that time. Don't request or allow the manager to return your call. Research studies have shown that when people are cold-calling, they have more success when a conversation takes place during a call that they initiated versus a call that was being returned.

If you must make a series of phone calls in order to reach the manager, try to get to know the secretary—this person can be an important ally. Introduce yourself and ask for his or her name; be friendly and try to engage the secretary in light conversation. By establishing a good rapport with this person, you may pave the way for a quick conversation with the manager, or be given a tip on the best time to call.

Once you're speaking with the manager, give a one- or two-sentence overview of your background and then explain that you would like to set up a meeting to discuss employment with his company.

If you have advance information that there's an opening, be sure to mention a related accomplishment (or responsibility) to demonstrate that you have the specific experience that the position requires.

As with the networking strategies, it's recommended that you practice these calls before making them. Also have notes in front of you. Some job-seekers take matters a step further. To ensure that they're proficient with this approach and don't lose out on any interviews, they first call managers at companies in which they have no interest in working. After an interview is scheduled, they call back and cancel it.

The following are the different responses you'll receive and the courses of action to take.

The manager asks you to send him a resume

Depending on the strength of your resume and the availability of free time, you will decide whether to send this document or describe your background in letter form. (If you have reservations about your resume, a hand-tailored letter will present your qualifications more convincingly and prevent you from being screened out.)

If you feel it would be advantageous to use a letter, explain that you're currently revising your resume but will immediately write a letter that outlines your experience. The manager won't object. He can ask for your resume at a later date should he need it.

Begin your correspondence by thanking the manager for the time he gave you. Next, state that a summary of your background follows, as per his request. Then present your experience in the broadcast letter format. Conclude by stating that you'll call in a few days to see when it might be convenient to meet.

If you elect to send a resume, enclose a cover letter that begins and concludes as the letter above.

In the event that you're pursuing a position that requires an excellent appearance and you have the desired image, it can be helpful to submit your correspondence in person (assuming the company is located nearby). When you give the receptionist the envelope, ask if the manager is available. You might be able to meet him at this time. If not, he could inquire about your appearance and the receptionist's comments will increase the likelihood of an interview. The receptionist might even volunteer this favorable information about you.

The manager asks you to send a resume to the personnel department

Decide whether to send your resume or a letter. (If you'll be using a letter to outline your background, inform the manager.) Then ask if you may send the manager a copy. Personnel is inundated with paperwork, and this guarantees that the manager will receive your correspondence in a timely fashion.

The manager tells you that he doesn't have an opening

Here most job-seekers make the error of thanking the manager for his time and ending the conversation. They forfeit the opportunity to develop leads and referrals.

Ask the manager if he knows of any companies that are looking for someone with your background. If he gives you a lead, ask for the name of the manager to contact. When you approach him, use this manager's name. This will give you credibility.

Before concluding the conversation, ask if you may send the manager your resume for future reference. This will enable him to contact you if a position opens up at his company.

The manager invites you in for an interview

This is the response you were hoping for. You will have uncovered an existing opening or interested the manager in creating one.

13. Telephoning Managers in Response to Advertisements

If you read an ad you want to answer, the first step is to see if you know someone at the company, or have a contact who does, who can arrange an introduction. As already discussed, the best way to meet a potential employer is through a referral.

If you don't know anyone who can arrange this meeting, the next step is to call the company and try to set up an interview with the hiring manager.

When an ad instructs you to contact a particular individual, but doesn't state his title or the department in which he works, call the company to find out what his responsibility is. He could be the hiring manager. If he is, have your call put through. If he's not, call back in a few hours and ask for the manager to whom this position would report (your objective is to bypass all individuals other than the hiring manager). When making this call, however, don't introduce yourself by name. While some managers will welcome your initiative and be eager to meet you, others will disapprove of your aggressiveness.

When an ad asks you to respond to someone in the personnel department, or just lists a telephone number, call the company and find out the name and title of the person to whom the position reports. Placing this call can be especially effective when an ad requests applicants to respond to a personnel representative. If you're successful in setting up the interview, you may be able to generate an offer before the manager even receives the resumes that are being sent to personnel. This situation is most likely to occur, however, with entry- and junior-level openings. This is where managers tend to make the quickest hiring decisions.

When you first speak with a manager, explain that you read the company's ad and believe you have the desired background, and ask for an interview. If the ad stated specific requirements, mention your pertinent strengths and accomplishments and/or responsibilities. If the ad was vague, describe your background in general terms. Always have the ad in front of you with notes to refer to.

The following are the different situations you'll encounter with suggested responses:

The manager asks you questions about your background

This indicates the manager is receptive to your call and might schedule an interview.

As you discuss your experience, ask the manager questions about the position in an effort to learn what its most important duties are. If you can obtain this information, you'll know which of your strengths, accomplishments, and responsibilities are most pertinent to the organization's needs. The sooner you bring forth these aspects of your background, the better your chances of setting up an interview.

Understand, however, that many managers won't be as cooperative as you would like. Because they haven't met you in person, they'll be reluctant to discuss the position in detail.

If the manager informs you that your experience isn't right for his current needs, ask if there's another department in the company that you can contact. Also ask if he knows of any other companies that might have appropriate openings. Then suggest sending your resume for future reference.

The manager asks you to send him a resume

Here, you must decide whether to write a letter or forward your resume.

Before agreeing to submit background information, however, tell the manager that you want to "confirm" that you have the specific experience he needs. Again, ask questions about the position to learn how to present your work history.

Whether you send a letter or a resume with a cover letter, begin your correspondence by making reference to this phone call and the manager's request for a summary of your background.

If you will be writing a letter, discuss your experience according to the position's requirements. (The way to outline your work history when answering an ad in letter form is explained in job-search strategy no. 17, "Responding to Newspaper Advertisements.") If you'll be sending your resume, your cover letter should provide a brief overview of your background as it relates to the position. Be sure to add any information not contained in your resume when you have learned that it will enhance your qualifications.

Conclude both letters by stating that you hope to hear back from the company or will be calling to follow up.

As in the previous job-search strategy, submit your correspondence in person if you think your appearance will advance your candidacy.

The manager asks you to send a resume to personnel

First, "confirm" that you have the type of experience the manager is looking for. Then advise him of the manner in which you'll be submitting your background, and ask if you may send him a copy of your correspondence.

The manager asks you to speak with the individual whose name appeared in the ad

Make this call, but don't mention that you contacted the manager.

Occasionally, an ad will state "No phone calls" or "Resumes only." Although these instructions frequently pertain to contacting the personnel department, it can still be risky calling a manager. Again, phone him without stating your name. You may be able to learn about the position without jeopardizing yourself.

As a general rule, if you haven't heard back from a company two weeks after mailing your response, place a follow-up phone call. There's no telling why you weren't contacted. Employers are deluged with resumes and applications, and it could be that your correspondence was misrouted or lost. In this instance, you now have the opportunity to resubmit your resume or letter. If the reason you didn't hear from the company was that there's something lacking in your background, you can now counter the objection.

So that you'll be able to handle any reservations about your qualifications, always keep copies of ads you have answered.

14. Telephoning Managers Who Have Recently Been Promoted or Who Have Moved to a New Company

This strategy is similar to job-search strategy no. 6, "Writing to Managers Who Have Recently Been Promoted or Who Have Moved to a New Company." The difference is that you place a phone call instead of sending a letter.

This call enables you to develop leads if a manager doesn't have an opening. In the case when a manager recently changed companies, he may have found his position through an extensive search of his own. He may know of openings for you at other organizations.

15. Telephoning the Previous Managers of People Who Have Recently Changed Companies

This strategy resembles job-search strategy no. 7, "Writing to the Previous Managers of People Who Have Recently Changed Companies." Again, the difference is calling on the phone instead of writing a letter, which also provides the opportunity to develop leads if a position isn't available.

16. Telephoning the Editors of Newsletters

If your goal is to work in a specific industry, it may be helpful to contact individuals who write newsletters about it. Their names, addresses, and telephone numbers can be obtained from the following sources: personnel departments of companies in the industry, employment agencies and executive search firms specializing in the industry (see pages 74–75 and 78–79 for the way to identify these recruiting firms), and the industry's trade associations and professional organizations. Also, read *The Standard Peri-*

odical Directory, Irregular Serials & Annuals, Ulrich's International Periodicals Directory, and *The Encyclopedia of Associations.* These publications list newsletters and their editors.

    Editors of newsletters will be of the most assistance to job-seekers who are pursuing management- and executive-level positions. Editors are often knowledgeable about the inner workings of the companies they write about and are privy to confidential, high-level staffing requirements.

Media Advertisements

These strategies include answering job advertisements that appear in newspapers and trade publications, as well as placing a "position wanted" notice of your own.

Reading ads is an easy way to identify job openings. Your responses will also be held in confidence since your background was solicited.

All organizations hire people through advertising, and you owe it to yourself to pursue these vacancies. Answering ads, however, has its share of problems.

You'll encounter considerable competition from other job-seekers. A large display ad in the *Wall Street Journal* or the Sunday edition of a major metropolitan newspaper can draw hundreds of replies.

The company that placed the ad will be utilizing other methods to recruit applicants. This increases the competition.

Organizations interview only 2% to 5% of the people who respond to their ads.

You have no control over the kinds of companies with which you can interview. It's up to chance that the type of position you want is being advertised by the kind of organization you wish to join.

The ads that appear aren't representative of the true number of openings. Companies advertise a mere 15% of their available positions.

Answering ads becomes less effective the higher the level of seniority. As positions increase in responsibility, companies shy away from advertising as a recruitment technique.

Last, the fact that an organization is running an ad doesn't mean that there's an opening. Ads are used for the purpose of taking salary surveys as well as to satisfy affirmative action requirements, even though the new employee has already been selected.

17. Responding to Newspaper Advertisements

Newspaper advertising is utilized by companies that are looking to hire people, as well as by executive search firms and employment agencies. Ads usually appear in the "Help Wanted" section of the Sunday edition, but they are occasionally placed in the business section as well.

Companies identify themselves in their ads and use the "blind box" approach. The latter is where they remain anonymous by omitting their names and addresses, giving a post office box number for response. To assure anonymity, they also provide a minimum of information about themselves and the position.

Executive search firms frequently place the blind box type of ad. It can therefore be difficult to distinguish their ads from those of companies. However, if an ad begins by stating, "We have been retained to find. . . " or "Our client has asked us to locate. . . ," the advertiser is clearly a search firm.

Employment agencies are usually required by state law to identify themselves as such. They use the following designations: "employment agency," "personnel consultants," "career consultants," "professional placement consultants," and "professional recruiters."

The overwhelming majority of ads is placed by companies. Utilization of the following procedures will increase the likelihood of obtaining interviews with these organizations.

An ad placed by a local company that identifies itself

As discussed in job-search strategy no. 13, "Telephoning Managers in Response to Advertisements," the first two steps to consider are approaching a company through a referral and calling the hiring manager on the phone. There are also two other courses of action:

You can respond by sending your background in letter form to the individual whose name appeared in the ad. Although this person could be the hiring manager, he's most likely to be in personnel or to be doing screening for the manager. In either case, his responsibility will be to review replies, so begin the letter by making reference to the ad. Cite the title of the position, name of the publication, and its date. Next, state your most significant accomplishment or responsibility in relation to the ad's requirements, including your title and type of employer. (As in a broadcast letter, your achievement and position need not have been with your current or most recent employer.) Then list additional accomplishments and/or duties in the order of their importance. Follow these achievements with a paragraph or two that provides other significant information. Conclude by stating that you hope to hear back from the company or will be calling to follow up.

Always omit salary information, even if it was requested. You don't want to be screened out because your earnings or income expectations are too high or too low.

The second approach is to call the company, find out the name and title of the hiring manager, and send this person an actual broadcast letter, just as if you were conducting a mass mailing. This will ensure that your background is read by the ultimate decision-maker. Be sure this letter doesn't mention the ad and that the envelope is marked "Personal & Confidential."

An ad placed by a company that identifies itself but is located out of town

Respond by sending a letter to the individual whose name appeared in the ad. Then, to ensure that your background will be read by the hiring manager, send him a broadcast letter. Since you probably won't want to incur the expense of calling the company to learn who this person is, obtain this information from the research publications in the library.

A blind box ad

Send a letter that begins by noting the ad. Then, if the position interests you enough, try to learn the identity of the company so that you can write to the hiring manager. There are several ways to find out who an advertiser is:

If the box number is with the U.S. Post Office, call the branch. You'll be given the name of the company. (The Post Office offers anonymity only to private individuals.)

If the box number is with a newspaper, call the paper. Some states require newspapers to identify an advertiser if requested.

Have a friend answer the ad according to job-search strategy no. 5, "Third-Party Correspondence." The letter must mention, however, that no fee is involved if the company interviews you or hires you. If the company responds, your friend will learn its identity.

Implement job-search strategy no. 11, "Providing a Post Office Box Number for Response."

Last, send the company a mailgram that states two or three outstanding accomplishments, but is signed with a name other than your own and furnishes a friend's address and phone number for contact information. If the company replies, your friend will advise the caller that the person who answered the ad isn't available at this time. He'll then obtain the company's name.

Answering a blind box ad provides a significant advantage: You'll have less competition from other job-seekers. Fewer people submit their background because so little information is provided. Many are also reluctant to respond for fear of who will learn of their interest in a new position—a particular concern of job-seekers who are currently employed.

When responding to newspaper advertisements, answer all ads where your background comes even close to meeting a company's requirements. If four prerequisites are listed and you can satisfy only two of them, contact the company. When organizations hire people, the new employees seldom have all the desired qualities.

The time that you mail your response is also a key consideration. Most job-seekers act immediately after the ad appears. This
quick reply actually works against them. At this time, companies
are often deluged with responses and are in a *screening-out* mode.
If you delay your reply, it will be more visible and receive that
much more attention. For entry-, junior-, and staff-level positions,
wait four days. At the management level, allow seven days. For
positions at the level of vice-president and above, delay action for
10 days.

An exception is when an ad appears to have been placed by a
small company. Because these kinds of organizations often make
hiring decisions very quickly, answer the ad at once.

As in job-search strategy no. 13, "Telephoning Managers in
Response to Advertisements," follow up on your correspondence
two weeks after having submitted your background if you haven't
been invited in for an interview.

This follow-up call will be most productive when the ad
instructed you to respond to the hiring manager. If you contact a
personnel representative, it will be more difficult to find out why
you weren't selected for an interview.

Answering ads can be effective when you want to relocate to a
specific part of the country. Read the leading newspaper in the
geographic area in which you want to work. This paper may even
contain an ad for a newsletter that lists openings in that region.

All newspapers offer short-term subscriptions. If you live in a
metropolitan area, you may be able to buy the paper from an out-
of-state news dealer or find it at the library.

The following newspapers are used extensively for advertising,
especially for management- and executive-level positions, regardless of a company's location: the *Wall Street Journal* (with four
regional editions: the Eastern, Midwest, Southwest, and Pacific
Coast), the *New York Times*, the *Chicago Tribune*, and the *Los
Angeles Times*. Also, *National Business Employment Weekly* contains all the "Positions Available" ads that appeared the previous
week in the four editions of the *Wall Street Journal*. *National*

Business Employment Weekly is sold at bookstores and at quality newsstands. You can take out either a short- or long-term subscription by writing to *National Business Employment Weekly*, P.O. Box 435, Chicopee, MA 01021-0435 or by calling (800) JOB-HUNT. (Along with featuring job advertisements, this publication provides excellent articles in each edition on the different parts of the job-search process and/or career development.)

When you answer ads, read back issues for up to eight weeks preceding the time you begin your search. It often takes companies months to fill a position, especially at the senior level.

In concluding the discussion on this strategy, it should be mentioned that you can also answer ads by sending companies your resume. This document, however, won't be as effective as an individually tailored letter. In addition, a resume should have a cover letter attached.* Thus, since you will have to write a letter anyway, you might as well compose the letter that will produce the most interviews—one that uses the broadcast letter format.

18. Responding to Trade Publication Advertisements

Most industries have trade magazines or newspapers. These publications contain "Help Wanted" sections for companies, executive search firms, and employment agencies to advertise their openings. This strategy is therefore an excellent vehicle for the job-seeker who wants to work in a specific industry.

To answer a trade publication advertisement, follow the same procedures that were described in job-search strategy no. 17, "Responding to Newspaper Advertisements."

---

* How to write this cover letter is explained on pages 99–100. The way to compose a resume is discussed on pages 85–98.

If you want to take out a short-term subscription, *The Standard Periodical Directory, All-in-One Directory, Standard Rate and Data Service Business Publications Directory,* and *The Encyclopedia of Business Information Sources* list, by specialty, the different publications and their addresses.

19. Responding to Advertisements with a Post Office Box Number

This strategy provides a way to answer ads while maintaining confidentiality as to your identity. It's also an appropriate means for responding to a blind box ad when you're concerned that the advertising company could be your own.

To implement the strategy, begin your correspondence by making reference to the ad. Then follow the same procedures for answering an ad placed by a local company that identifies itself. (See job-search strategy no. 17, "Responding to Newspaper Advertisements.") Conclude, however, by stating that it's because you're in the same industry as the advertiser that you must initially remain anonymous. The letter will be unsigned and furnish a post office box number for response.

Because you're omitting your name, this type of reply will generate fewer interviews than had you identified yourself. For this reason, this approach shouldn't be used unless you have superb qualifications for the position that's being advertised.

20. Responding to Advertisements via Third-Party Correspondence

Another way to maintain confidentiality is to have a friend answer the ad in your behalf.

The letter should begin by noting the ad.

Next, your sponsor should state that he's writing for a highly qualified individual, citing your title and type of employer, who wishes to remain anonymous because he's in the same industry as the advertiser.

Your strengths, accomplishments, and responsibilities will then be listed, in the order of their importance and in the broadcast letter format. A paragraph can also be included to furnish additional pertinent information.

The letter should conclude by stating that the writer will put the company in touch with the individual he's representing and that no fee will be charged for this service.

Again, this type of response will produce fewer interviews than had you answered the ad yourself. However, if your sponsor holds a key position with a company in the same industry as the advertiser, he should cite his title and the name of his employer. (In this instance, it isn't necessary to state that a fee won't be charged for arranging the introduction.) This will give him credibility and increase your number of interviews.

Responding to ads via third-party correspondence is preferable to using a post office box number. It also eliminates the expense of taking out the post office box and the inconvenience of picking up mail.

21. Placing a "Position Wanted" Advertisement

This strategy consists of advertising your qualifications and availability in various media. Appropriate publications are trade magazines, newsletters, the classified and business sections of a Sunday newspaper, the *National Business Employment Weekly*, and the *Wall Street Journal*.

Most publications run a column titled "Positions Wanted" for this purpose. If you select the *Wall Street Journal*, Tuesday is the best day to run an ad, since the paper runs a special column, "Positions Wanted," on that day.

The ad should state the position you're seeking and briefly list your key qualifications. Its size need not be more than 5 to 10 one-column lines.

Although this isn't a preferred strategy, it occasionally brings results. Unfortunately, you may receive more responses from employment agencies and retail outplacement firms than from companies wanting to arrange interviews.

This approach can be of assistance to the job-seeker who wants to work in a specific part of the country, particularly if he has a background that's in great demand but is difficult to find. Placing an ad can also be used when the objective is to work in a particular industry; in this case it's best to advertise in trade publications.

Registration

Registration is presenting your background to organizations that can provide you with interviews or leads for job openings.

As with answering ads, these strategies are inexpensive and require little effort on your part. They also have the same drawback: It's a matter of chance whether or not you obtain an interview for the position you want with the kind of organization you desire. A statistic underscoring this point is that companies list only 5% of the openings that they have with employment agencies. They advise other organizations of an even smaller percentage of their vacancies.

22. Employment Agencies

Of all the methods job-seekers use to generate interviews, working with employment agencies is the most poorly handled and least understood. Many people are suspicious of agencies and work with them as a last resort. Others won't have anything to do with these firms at all.

The truth of the matter is that for some job-seekers registering with employment agencies is one of the most effective ways to obtain interviews. It also requires little time and often no financial outlay (there are many firms where the employer pays the fee). In fact, if you handle agencies properly, these firms will spend their time and their money working for you.

Before we discuss the procedures to follow, here's how an agency operates:

The individuals working at employment agencies are hired on a commission basis. As a result, they are under considerable pressure "to place" people, to find them jobs. When they think they can do this quickly and easily, they accept someone as an applicant. Otherwise, they don't give people any time at all. This is borne out by the fact that employment agencies arrange interviews for only 1 out of every 20 job-seekers who contact them. In addition, when agencies set up appointments, they often have little concern for how closely a position matches someone's objectives. They select situations where they believe offers will be made; then they press for an acceptance. Their predominant concern is to get someone hired and earn a commission.

This is the environment you walk into when you visit an agency. It isn't appealing, but you can take certain measures that will prevent your being treated this way. These same measures will enable you to realize the maximum results that agencies can provide.

Once you have met your agency representative, set the tone for the relationship by explaining the specific position you're seeking, your qualifications for it, and the kinds of situations you want to avoid.

Don't volunteer that you're using other resources to develop interviews, especially that you're working with other agencies. The less competition this individual thinks he has, the harder he'll work in your behalf.

If you're asked which companies you have seen, never mention ones in which you're interested, particularly where offers might be forthcoming. Your agency representative might take this information, call the companies, and try to fill these positions with his other applicants.

Finally, establish who pays the fee. With some agencies it will be the company. With others it will be you. If the fee will be your responsibility, make sure you understand the amount, the terms of payment, and the agency's guarantee policy.

Once you have established these ground rules you'll be able to capitalize on your agency representative's knowledge of the job market and his desire to place you. If he has the kinds of openings you're looking for, he'll arrange interviews. Otherwise he'll inform you that these positions aren't on file, and he won't waste your time trying to interest you in others.

If your agency contact feels that you're especially qualified for the position you want, he might take matters a step further. He may conduct a dedicated search in your behalf, where he'll call a host of possible employers and present your background. He can also do this without revealing your identity, if you happen to require anonymity.

Although this dedicated search will result in interviews, don't rely on it for all the exposure you want. Many companies don't work with employment agencies, and when they do, they work with a select number of firms. As a result, each agency can represent you to only a limited number of companies.

Deciding which agencies to use is an important consideration. There are several ways to determine this:

Ask your friends to recommend agencies with which they've had success. Also ask them to introduce you to the individual with whom they worked. This referral will help you become the 1 applicant out of 20 who obtains interviews.

Read the *Yellow Pages* under "Employment Agencies." These firms often list the fields in which they specialize. Visit the appropriate agencies or send them your resume.* A cover letter is suggested, but not required. You'll be contacted if an agency thinks it can place you.

Many agencies advertise openings in the "Help Wanted" section of Sunday newspapers. If a firm lists only one position of

----

* A resume is recommended instead of a letter because some companies require agencies to furnish this document before they will schedule interviews.

interest, call to discuss the job. If several positions are advertised, however, this indicates that the agency specializes in the industry or field and a personal visit is warranted.

If your objective is to work in a particular industry or field, read the appropriate trade publications. Agencies that specialize in your area of interest will advertise in these media. Call the firms that are local and send your resume to the others.

If the geographic region in which you want to live has an abundance of companies in your specialty, you'll find agencies that concentrate in your line of work. For example, agencies specialize in the computer industry in the San Francisco Peninsula and along Route 128 outside Boston; in the pharmaceutical industry in New Jersey; and in the advertising industry in New York City.

To identify the agencies to approach, call the personnel departments at a few of the companies in the industry or field. Ask for their recommendations, including the names of the best people to contact.

Last, there are two publications to consider: *Directory of Executive Recruiters* lists the prominent agencies throughout the country. The firms are categorized geographically as well as by the industries and job functions in which they concentrate. You can purchase a copy from Kennedy Publications, 2 Kennedy Way, Fitzwilliam, NH 03447 ([800] 531-0007). *The Recruiting & Search Report* lists agencies as well. There are four regional editions, and agencies are also grouped by job category and industry of specialization. Write to P.O. Box 9433, Panama City Beach, FL 32417 or call (800) 634-4548.

The results you obtain from an agency will depend on the ability of the individual who represents you. If you feel this person is inexperienced or doesn't understand your qualifications and objective, speak to the manager and ask to be assigned to someone else. Agencies are plagued by personnel turnover and are constantly training new people. You don't want to have a trainee working on your search. Also, if your agency representative isn't producing interviews for you, call him once a week "just to stay in touch." He's always hearing about new positions, and this call will assure that he remembers you.

If your objective is to relocate to a specific part of the country, send your resume to the agencies in that geographic area. To identify these firms, read *Directory of Executive Recruiters, The Recruiting & Search Report,* the *Yellow Pages,* and the "Help Wanted" sections of the appropriate Sunday newspapers. Contact as many agencies as you can. Fifty is not too many.

Working with employment agencies isn't an effective strategy for all job-seekers. These firms usually place people in entry-, junior-, and staff-level positions. This is where there are the most openings, the greatest turnover, and their best chances of success.

However, if you can find an agency that *specializes* in your industry or job function, then it may be of assistance to you even if you hold a senior-staff or management-level responsibility. The employment agency business has matured to the point that today there are individuals in it who have the expertise of executive recruiters. They also place people in jobs paying up to $75,000 per year. In addition, client companies always assume the fee.

Never rule out an agency because it's located far away. When an agency specializes in an industry or field, its clients are often national in scope.

Agencies are especially effective for certain types of job-seekers: recent college graduates, secretaries, general office personnel, sales representatives, engineers, computer programmers and analysts, accountants, and financial analysts. Many firms specialize in placing these types of individuals and will arrange interviews for them within minutes of having learned about their backgrounds. If you fit one of these categories, visiting agencies should be one of the first strategies you consider using.

23. Trade Associations and Professional Organizations

Sometimes companies list openings with the trade associations and professional organizations that serve their industries. These groups act as no-fee clearing houses between their corporate and individual members. You can advise these organizations of your interest in setting up interviews by sending them a letter or your resume with a cover letter attached.

Some trade associations and professional organizations publish newsletters that announce current openings. Ask to be put on the mailing list.

When companies utilize these organizations for recruitment assistance, they're usually seeking specific industry experience. However, because skills can be transferable from one industry to another, this strategy is often effective for the job-seeker who wants to enter a particular industry.

If there's a national association or organization that has a local chapter in your area, or if there's an independent group that's local, contact the president and try to arrange a personal meeting. This person will be an invaluable source for referrals.

24. Executive Search Firms

In order to fill high-level positions, companies often retain executive search firms to identify and recruit individuals with specific kinds of experience. These positions usually command salaries of at least $75,000 and are at the level of manager and above. Executive search firms will therefore be of use to a minority of job-seekers. These firms will also do nothing to find someone a position. They work strictly for their corporate clients.

If you're at this management or salary level, you should give strong consideration to sending executive search firms your resume. This is the only strategy that doesn't decrease in effectiveness as a job-seeker's level of seniority increases. In fact, it's estimated that companies fill 25% of their management-level openings through these firms. When writing to search organizations, always attach a cover letter to your resume.

If your experience is appropriate for a current assignment, you'll be contacted for an interview. Otherwise, executive search firms will retain your resume in their files and call you when an appropriate position arises.

When you write these firms, it isn't necessary to address any particular person by name and title. However, if you have a contact who is held in high regard by a certain firm, ask him to arrange an introduction. This referral will give you credibility, and when your background is selected for an assignment, you'll be viewed as a preferred prospect.

Unfortunately, the likelihood is remote that a firm will be looking for someone with your background at the time you initiate contact. For this reason, write to between 50 and 100 executive recruiters.

If your objective is to relocate to a particular part of the country, it's best to approach firms located in that area, since these organizations *tend* to work on openings near their offices. (This is especially the case with the smaller firms.) However, positions can actually be anywhere in the country (or in the world for that matter) because clients are often national and international in scope, with subsidiaries, divisions, and plants canvassing the globe.

If you see an ad placed by a search firm, and the organization is local, call to arrange an interview. Otherwise, send a letter that begins by noting the ad.*

---

* Since you know that the firm is currently looking for a specific type of background as well as what the key requirements are, this letter will enable you to tailor your experience accordingly.

To identify executive search firms, see the *Directory of Executive Recruiters*, which lists organizations throughout the country, including the minimum salary levels at which they work and the industries and job functions in which they concentrate. This publication cross-indexes these firms by industry and job function as well. You can also order a copy of *The Recruiting & Search Report*; there are four regional editions, with groupings according to industry and job function. In addition, the *Yellow Pages* lists search firms under "Executive Search Firms." (A few, unfortunately, will really be employment agencies.)

25. The Alumni Placement Office

Companies sometimes list openings with college and university alumni placement offices. These departments serve two functions: (1) they maintain job banks of current listings, and (2) they match graduates' resumes against these openings and forward them to the appropriate companies.

Sending a resume to your alumni placement office presents three problems. First, there's no confidentiality. Not only are company recruiters free to review the resumes that are on file, but you have no control over the companies that will be sent your background. Second, companies tend to utilize this recruitment source for junior- and staff-level positions. An exception, though, is the alumni placement office for graduate programs. Here, companies list high-level openings. Third, positions are seldom located in the geographic area in which you want to work.

Some alumni placement offices also maintain a databank, categorized by industry, of where graduates are currently employed. This will provide valuable leads, since alumni are receptive to hearing from others and like to help with a networking process.

26. Forty Plus Clubs

Forty Plus Clubs are nonprofit organizations in which members assist one another in finding new employment. In order to join, you must be a U.S. citizen, unemployed, and at least 40 years old. An initial fee and monthly contribution are required. A member must also devote a specified number of hours to club activities each week.

These organizations act as support groups where members share job openings, arrange interviews for one another, provide contacts, and offer assistance in matters such as resume-writing and interviewing techniques.

To find the nearest branch, write to Forty Plus Clubs, 15 Park Row, New York, NY 10038.

27. The College Placement Office

This strategy is one of the most effective ways for the graduating college student to develop interviews. It provides three advantages. First, the student selects the companies with which he wants to interview. Second, he's assured that an opening is at the entry level and that no previous work experience is required. Third, his educational background will always be respected by a potential employer.

Some college placement offices also maintain a databank, categorized by industry, of where its alumni work. This will provide excellent leads. The databank can be used by alumni as well.

28. Job Fairs

Job fairs are events where employers rent booths or rooms at a central location to meet with local residents who are looking for work. The employers are usually from the immediate area and they often hold these functions at a community center, hotel, or school. Frequently they're seeking specific types of backgrounds and have multiple openings for each position. These events are therefore not for individuals pursuing management- and executive-level responsibilities.

Job fairs are advertised in the classified section of Sunday newspapers. Many are also listed in *National Business Employment Weekly*'s "Calendar of Events" section (sometimes they are advertised as well).

A job fair presents the opportunity to meet with many different companies within a short period of time. It's like doing one-stop shopping. Because it's so easy to talk to people, it's also an excellent way to network. Due to the visibility job-seekers have, though, it's seldom appropriate for people who are currently employed.

If you go to a job fair, bring plenty of copies of your resume. Also get business cards from the company representatives you speak with, and write them thank-you letters the next day. (How to write a thank-you letter is explained in Section Four, page 161.)

Although the atmosphere at a job fair will be casual and informal, always dress and act professionally. Remember that you're really at a job interview.

29. On-Line Job-Listing Services

If you have a computer with a modem (or have access to one), you can subscribe to a computer-based service that lists job openings. Also known as *computer bulletin boards*, these job lists are provided by professional societies, trade associations, trade publications, government agencies, college placement offices, and commercial electronic database companies. Often the positions that are listed have never been advertised. They may also be located anywhere in the country.

Sometimes there's no charge for the use of this service, except for routine charges from your telephone company. Commercial operators, however, always charge an access fee, usually around

$50 for a three-month period of time. Some organizations require that you be a member before you can use their service.

Many services list jobs in only one industry or field. Others offer jobs in up to as many as two dozen different occupational categories. A few operators of bulletin boards also list jobs according to geographic area, and/or accept resumes electronically and then fax them to potential employers.

If you think you might want to try one of these services, find out how often its list is updated. The more current the information, the less downtime you'll have pursuing positions that are no longer available. There's often a delay between the time a company fills a position and when it notifies the operator of this situation.

To find out the organizations that provide these services, contact Coastal Associates Publishing, 1 Park Ave., New York, NY 10016 ([212] 503-3500). Each month this company publishes "The Computer Shopper," which describes bulletin boards throughout the country. These job lists are sorted by telephone area code.

Three of the largest commercial job-listing services are:

kiNexus's Career Network
640 LaSalle St., Suite 560
Chicago, IL 60610
(800) 229-6499

E-Span JobSearch
8440 Woodfield Crossing, Suite 170
Indianapolis, IN 46240
(800) 682-2901

CompuServe Bulletin Board
5000 Arlington Centre Blvd.
Columbus, OH 43220
(614) 457-8600

30. Resume Databases

Resume databases are operated by companies that take basic information from your resume and input it into their electronic database. Employers that are on-line clients of these services then access the database and ask for certain characteristics. When your background contains the traits an employer is seeking, you'll be contacted for more information and possibly an interview. Some operators of resume databases will also review their files and perform this search function for companies that are not on-line clients.

Annual fees for this service range from as little as $25 to several hundred dollars, often depending on how many job or industry categories you wish to be listed under in the database. Some firms charge a one-time fee that entitles you to a lifetime membership.

A potential problem with this job-hunting technique is its lack of confidentiality. Some services, however, are able to put you on their database and withhold your name, address, and telephone number.

If you want to try this approach, ask the operator of the database how many employers are using it as well as how many resumes have been reviewed during the past 12 months. This is a new service and you might find that there aren't enough organizations participating in it to make it worth your while. Likewise, many companies feel that there aren't enough job candidates on a database to make it useful to them. Also find out what industries or fields the employers are in, the size of these companies, and where they are located.

Here are some of the largest resume databases in the country (this information was made available by *National Business Employment Weekly*):

Career Placement Registry Inc.
3202 Kirkwood Highway
Wilmington, DE 19808
(800) 331-4955

Corporate Organizing and Research Services
One Pierce Place
Itasca, IL 60143
(800) 323-1352

Datamation Databank
265 S. Main St.
Akron, OH 44308
(800) 860-2252

Job Bank USA
1420 Spring Hill Rd.
McLean, VA 22102
(800) 296-1872

kiNexus, Inc.
640 LaSalle St., Suite 560
Chicago, IL 60610
(800) 828-0422

National Employee Database
418 Ashmun St.
Sault Ste. Marie, MI 49783
(800) 366-3633

SkillSearch
104 Woodmont Blvd.
Nashville, TN 37205
(800) 258-6641

Other Considerations

How to Write a Winning Resume

Certain job-search strategies require the use of a resume. In the discussion that follows, you'll learn how to present your background so that you'll convincingly convey your qualifications for the position you're seeking.

The value of writing a resume, however, goes far beyond producing a tool for generating interviews. Through the process of composing this document, you'll gain a clear picture of how you want to present yourself with potential employers, especially what to emphasize and play down from your background. As a result, you'll make a more persuasive presentation and be better equipped to convert interviews into offers.

Writing a resume also presents two challenges. The first is to make the document as brief as possible, but not at the expense of omitting vital information. The shorter the length (one page is preferred; however, two are acceptable), the greater the likelihood that your resume will be read. Interviewers balk at having to sift through reams of data in order to learn what an applicant has to offer. Lengthy resumes are often automatically filed away and the applicants are eliminated from consideration.

The second challenge is to describe your background so that your resume paints the most inviting picture possible of your qualifications. Although you can't change the facts about your background, you can present them in such a way that your resume highlights the most important points about your experience and plays down—or even omits—any negative factors. Clearly, most job-seekers have circumstances in their backgrounds that they wish were not brought out by their resume.

In the following pages, you'll learn how to meet both of these challenges and create a resume that will achieve the results you want.

Preparing Your Resume

Your resume has one purpose—to convey your qualifications for the position you're seeking—and it achieves this in a specific way, by highlighting those *strengths*, *accomplishments*, and *responsibilities* that will demonstrate your ability to perform this job. Here's how to proceed:

Begin by stating your job objective

Your job objective is one of the most important parts of your resume. It plays two key roles:

First of all, it determines the *content* of your resume—the specific information that will be included, emphasized, played down, and even omitted. Your job objective is like a rudder—it steers you through the process of deciding what to say about your background so that you'll convincingly set forth your qualifications for the position you want.

Second, the presence of your job objective increases the likelihood of generating interviews. Employers are accustomed to seeing this statement on a resume, and when it doesn't appear many believe that the job-hunter lacks career direction. This hurts their chances of being selected for an interview.

In addition, resumes often receive no more than a 15- to 30-second scan, especially when someone is performing an initial screening function and has to comb through dozens or even hundreds of these documents. By stating your job objective, you make it easy for the screener to forward your resume to the proper manager. This is particularly the case at large companies where there are many managers to choose from.

Due to the importance of your job objective, exercise great care when wording it. On one hand, you want it to be specific so that people will know exactly what it is that you want to do. On the other hand, you don't want your job objective to be so narrow that you can be eliminated from closely related positions. If you have several job targets in mind—and they are diverse in their tasks and responsibilities—it's best to write a separate resume for each one.

Use "Job Objective" for the title of this section.

Presenting your educational background

When your education relates to your job objective, this information should appear next. When your education is unrelated, it should be presented toward the end of your resume after you've described your work background. This will allow prospective employers to get right to your work experience, which will set forth your key strengths, accomplishments, and responsibilities.

If you have a college degree, or hold a two-year degree from a community college, cite the degree, your major, the college you attended, and the year in which you were graduated. Also include any honors, awards, or scholarships you received as well as your G.P.A. (grade point average) or class standing, if they were favorable. Always omit high school education.

In the event that you hold an advanced degree (or are currently studying for one), include this information by citing the degree, the name of the college, and the graduation date (or expected graduation date). This information should appear before your undergraduate degree.

If you lack a degree but have some college or community college experience, list the school you attended (or are attending), courses you've taken that pertain to your job objective, and dates of matriculation.

If you have no college experience at all, state the high school you attended, its location by city and state, and year of graduation.

In addition, list any other educational experiences *that pertain to your job objective*. These can include courses taken at a vocational school as well as correspondence courses, evening classes, company-sponsored training, seminars, workshops, and conferences.

This section is almost always titled "Education."

Describing your work experience

Your work experience can be presented in two different ways: the *chronological* format (turn to page 34 for an example) or the *functional-chronological* format (see page 96 for an example).

The chronological format

In this type of resume, you discuss your work background in reverse chronological order, detailing all your employers, their locations by city and state, your dates of employment, your job titles, and then your key accomplishments and responsibilities.

Elaborate on the jobs where your activities are the most pertinent to your job objective. Say little, if anything, about your other assignments. This way prospective employers will focus on your strengths and qualifications. In the event that you've held more than one position at a company, concentrate on the job that's the most important.

List your accomplishments in the order in which they will present the strongest case for your capability. Also begin each one with an "action" word (don't begin by stating, "I. . .") and use *numbers* to convey their *extent*. (See page 97 for a list of "action" words.) In addition, indent your accomplishments and precede each one with a dash if your resume will be typewritten and then photocopied, or with a bullet if your resume will be professionally printed. This type of layout will make your accomplishments stand out.

When thinking about your different activities and accomplishments, be sure to include anything you've done that was new and different or, more important, innovative and resourceful. Also state the specific benefit the company derived from your work.

If your background is administrative and doesn't lend itself to visible accomplishments, then state your *responsibilities*, indicating their scope when possible. For example, cite the number of people or forms you processed each day, the dollar volume of the project you worked on, or the size of the facility, department, or company at which you worked.

When discussing responsibilities, it's acceptable to do so in a paragraph instead of in separate sentences preceded by a dash or bullet. Responsibilities are usually less dramatic than accomplishments and therefore don't warrant this special treatment.

In the event that you haven't worked in many years and are now reentering the work force, include any relevant part-time jobs or volunteer work. If you're a recent college graduate or have only a few years of experience, cite any part-time jobs and summer employment. Also note the portion of your education you may have paid for.

Titles for this section include "Experience," "Work Experience," "Professional Experience," and "Work Background."

The chronological format is best for job-seekers whose experience consists of progressive growth into positions of increased responsibility, since this format automatically emphasizes growth. Also, due to the prominence of employers' names, the format will highlight the fact that you've worked for prestigious companies, if this was the case.

The chronological approach can also present certain problems. First of all, if your current or most recent position doesn't directly relate to your job objective, you may instantly be disqualified as a candidate. Employers usually prefer to hire people who are currently performing closely related work, since this will enable them to make an immediate contribution. This is a particular problem for job-seekers who are trying to *change careers* as well as for individuals whose pertinent experience appears toward the end of their resume. Often, these people's resumes aren't read in their entirety and employers fail to learn about their qualifications. (The functional-chronological format will prevent this situation from occurring.)

Second, this format may force you to include experiences you would prefer not to mention, such as a reduction in responsibilities or having held positions that are unrelated to your job objective.

Third, because the chronological format includes dates of employment, it will reveal periods of unemployment and job-hopping, as well as the fact that you have spent only a short amount of time in a certain position, should any of these be the case.

The functional-chronological format

In this format, you discuss your accomplishments and responsibilities according to *function*, or type of activity performed, and then state your employment history in reverse chronological order. Including job titles is optional. Since the functional headings immediately call attention to your strengths, it's less important to use bullets or dashes to highlight your accomplishments.

There are four advantages to the functional-chronological format:

First, you can instantly set forth any part of your background (the experience may be buried in a chronological resume).

Second, you can convey that you have expertise in *several* functional areas. For example, you can highlight a dual capability in any of the following: administration, data processing, engineering, finance, manufacturing, marketing, research and development, or sales; or you can include a knowledge of a particular industry, product line, or service, or the fact that you have a particular set of skills in a certain area. This latitude is especially useful to senior-level job-seekers who have both breadth and depth of experience.

Third, because the format begins with strengths and accomplishments, it diminishes the impact of liabilities such as job-hopping and periods of unemployment. These shortcomings aren't noted until after qualifications have been clearly established.

Fourth, the format will conceal a history of unrelated positions, a background that is frowned upon by employers since it demonstrates a lack of career direction.

The functional-chronological format is especially effective for job-seekers who want to make a *career change,* since it doesn't start with their most recent experience, which is usually inapplicable, as the chronological format does. Career-changers can also highlight those parts of their backgrounds that would usually appear toward the end of a chronological resume—such as community activities and hobbies—when they would demonstrate their qualifications for the position they're pursuing.

Additional information

After you have presented your work experience, use any of the following sections when they will provide information that will support your ability to perform your job objective: "Professional Organizations," "Trade Associations," "Community Activities," "Awards," "Honors," "Commendations," "Inventions," "Patents," "Licenses," "Certifications," "Copyrights," "Publications," "Foreign Languages," "Hobbies," and "Military Experience." Including a "Personal" section is optional.

If there's something important about your background that you wish to include, but the information doesn't fit into one of these categories, provide this data in a section titled "Comments."

Concluding your resume with the statement "References furnished on request" is optional.

If your resume takes up two full pages or more, it's recommended that you add a special section titled "Summary," "Career Summary," or "Profile." This section should appear immediately after "Job Objective," and its purpose is to summarize your expertise to ensure that your resume will be read in its entirety. A two- or three-sentence summary will suffice. This section is especially important when using the chronological format, since key experience might not be readily visible. You can also list important personal traits in this summary statement.

Had Jack Bartello's resume been lengthy, he would have written:

CAREER SUMMARY	A track record of accomplishments in marketing industrial chemical products as a sales manager, sales trainer, and key account sales representative. Experience includes end-user as well as distributor sales. Resourceful, an excellent communicator, highly motivated, the ability to motivate others.

A Special Word for Career-Changers

Many people who want to change careers actually have the required skills, but lack the work experience to substantiate that they have these talents. This problem can be overcome by adding a section to your resume that lists these skills. For example, if someone wants to be a sales representative but has never sold before, the job-hunter would use the functional-chronological format and then add the following section:

SALES SKILLS	• An outstanding communicator • Relate well with different types of people • A convincing personality • Highly motivated • Possess stamina, perseverance, and excellent follow-through

Overcoming Liabilities: Periods of Unemployment and Your Age

Periods of Unemployment

Short gaps in employment are easy to conceal, in both the chronological and functional-chronological formats. Instead of stating employment dates in *months and years*, cite *years only*. Notice that this is what Jack Bartello did.

In the event that you have a period of unemployment that lasts *several years*, you can mask this by not providing dates of employment, and, instead, stating the *number of years* you have worked for an employer. Using Jack Bartello's background as an example, a job-hunter would state:

Alexa Chemicals Co., Boston, MA. (2 years)
Erving Real Estate, St. Louis, MO. (1 year)
Malone Chemicals, Inc., Philadelphia, PA. (1 year)
Faucet Construction Co., Orlando, FL. (1 year)

Granted, this second approach will arouse suspicion among potential employers since they're used to seeing dates of employment on a resume. However, you'll have a better chance of generating interviews using this approach versus leaving no doubt about your periods of unemployment.

Age
If you prefer not to reveal your age, use the functional-chronological format, and in the "Employment History" section cite the number of years you have worked for each company (as was done above).

This approach won't work, however, if you have a degree, since your date of graduation will indicate your age (unless you received your degree well after you began your career). In this instance, put your educational background *after* your work experience and leave out the graduation date. With your qualifications clearly established, some employers might not be disturbed by the fact that this date is missing. Some will be suspicious, though.

Unfortunately, there's nothing you can do in a resume to cover up job-hopping. If you try to achieve this by omitting dates altogether, or the amount of time you worked for companies, you will cause so much concern that the likelihood of developing interviews will be practically nil.

Once you're meeting with an employer, the above liabilities will invariably surface during the course of conversation. However, because you're now face-to-face with an interviewer, you have the opportunity to offer good explanations for periods of unemployment as well as your reasons for having left certain companies. (This information should never appear in a resume.) If these liabilities were visible on your resume, you might never have been able to set up the interview in the first place.

Reviewing Your Resume

Once you have finished the first draft of your resume, review what you have written and ask yourself the following questions: "Does this resume highlight my strengths and accomplishments and demonstrate my ability to perform my job objective?" "What negatives are brought out?" "What changes can I make to minimize their impact?" and "What changes can I make to strengthen my qualifications?"

For each piece of information you've offered, ask yourself: "What does this say about me?" "What does this *not* say about me?" and "What does this imply?" Make the required changes. Rewrite your resume as many times as necessary. Always be checking for spelling, grammar, and punctuation.

Once you're satisfied with your resume, show it to your friends. Ask for their comments and suggestions for improvement. The document may not read to others as it does to you. You will get the most useful feedback from people who are knowledgeable about your field.

Resume Appearance

The appearance of your resume is as important as its content. If the document is overrun with words or has a poor visual effect, it might not be read at all.

So that your resume will be attractive to the eye, make sure there's a good deal of "white space." There should be one inch from the top and from the bottom, as well as at the left and right margins. There should also be ample spacing between the different sections.

If your resume is going to be typewritten and photocopied, use an electric typewriter. Also, test the photocopier to make sure it doesn't leave blemishes or dots, due to a dirty glass.

If your resume will be professionally printed (this is the preferred method), try to select a layout and type size that will allow the document to be one page in length. Don't use such small type, however, that a reader will have to squint—a two-page resume is just fine. Also, choose a conservative style to lend dignity to your resume. Exotic type is usually frowned upon, except for job-seekers who are in artistic fields.

Select good-quality 8½" × 11" stock. Recommended colors are ivory, light beige, and light gray. Have matching envelopes printed with your return address. Also purchase stationery for your cover letters.

Always proofread the printer's work, since it's rare for mistakes not to be made. Also, do the proofreading at home, not in the printer's office. The task is harder than it appears because the tendency is to read complete words, not individual letters. If you read your resume *backwards,* you'll catch errors you would otherwise miss. Proofread for layout as well as for spelling and punctuation.

Jack P. Bartello
115 Navarre St.
Hyde Park, MA 02136
(617) 361-0576

OBJECTIVE   Sales Manager, Sales Training Manager, or Key Account Sales
Representative for a large company manufacturing chemicals or industrial
products.

EDUCATION   B.S., Chemistry, Rollins College, 1987.

CAREER SUMMARY

SALES   Complete responsibility for managing the sales of industrial chemicals in
MANAGEMENT the 6 New England states. Increased sales 75% and brought the region
from #7 in the country to #2 within 2 years.

SALES   Created sales training/motivation programs that contributed significantly to
TRAINING   the above sales increase; these programs were adopted by the company
on a national basis. Have trained new hires who were quickly promoted to
district sales responsibilities. Have also trained distributors' sales
personnel.

SALES   Experience includes selling industrial chemical products to distributors and
end-users. Increased dollar volume with existing customers and
performed extensive prospecting to bring in new customers. Developed
several new customers to National Key Account status in less than 1 year.
Have increased sales as much as 50% within 1½ years. Customer
base has consisted of Fortune 500 companies, small businesses, colleges
and universities, and municipalities. Account call has included all levels,
from executive to purchasing.

EMPLOYMENT Alexa Chemicals Co., Boston, MA. 1991–1993. Regional Sales Manager.
HISTORY   Erving Real Estate, St. Louis, MO. 1990–1991. Sales Agent.
Malone Chemicals, Inc., Philadelphia, PA. 1989–1990. District Sales
    Representative.
Faucet Construction Co., Orlando, FL. 1988–1989. Inside Salesman.

COMMUNITY   Big Brothers of America, The United Way.
ACTIVITIES

PERSONAL   Married with 2 children, excellent health.

References furnished on request.

Action Words

accelerated
accounted for
achieved
acted
adapted
addressed
administered
advertised
adopted
advanced
advised
aligned
analyzed
anticipated
arbitrated
appraised
approved
arranged
ascertained
assembled
assessed
assigned
attained
audited
augmented
automated
budgeted
built
calculated
cared for
charted
checked
classified
collected

communicated
compiled
completed
composed
conceived of
conceptualized
conducted
consolidated
constructed
consulted
contracted
contributed to
controlled
convinced
coordinated
counseled
created
danced
debated
decided
decorated
decreased
defined
delegated
demonstrated
designed
detected
determined
developed
devised
diagnosed
directed
discovered
displayed

disproved
diverted
drafted
drew
edited
effected
eliminated
enforced
enhanced
enlarged
enlisted
established
estimated
evaluated
examined
exhibited
expanded
expedited
experimented
explained
fabricated
facilitated
financed
fixed
formulated
founded
gathered
generated
guided
handled
headed
hypnotized
identified
illustrated

implemented	painted	restructured
improved	participated in	revamped
increased	perceived	reviewed
influenced	performed	revised
informed	persuaded	saved
initiated	planned	scheduled
innovated	predicted	selected
inspired	prepared	separated
installed	prescribed	set up
instituted	presented	served
instructed	prioritized	serviced
integrated	processed	shaped
interpreted	produced	sketched
invented	projected	sold
investigated	promoted	solved
judged	proposed	sorted
launched	proved	spearheaded
lectured	provided	spoke
led	publicized	started
maintained	published	streamlined
managed	purchased	strengthened
manufactured	questioned	structured
mediated	realigned	studied
modeled	recommended	summarized
molded	reconciled	supervised
monitored	recorded	supported
motivated	reduced	surveyed
navigated	rehabilitated	synchronized
negotiated	reinforced	synergized
observed	reorganized	synthesized
operated	repaired	systematized
ordered	reported	tabulated
organized	researched	taught
originated	resolved	tested
oversaw	restored	trained

transcribed	*unified*	*was promoted*
translated	*united*	*won*
transmitted	*upgraded*	*wrote*
triggered	*verbalized*	
trouble-shot	*was awarded*	

The Resume Cover Letter

Although every effort has been made to explain the advantage of approaching a potential employer through a letter and to encourage you to do so, sending a resume is a viable alternative. Your resume, however, should be accompanied by a cover letter.

The absence of a cover letter is in poor taste and will make an unfavorable impression. This letter is more than a formality, though. It allows you to explain your reason for contacting the company as well as highlight an important aspect of your background. As discussed earlier, you can also use this letter to include information that doesn't appear in your resume when you've learned that it will strengthen your qualifications.

Cover Letter for Answering an Advertisement

The type of salutation you use will depend on what was stated in the ad. If an individual's name was listed, write to him by name and title. Otherwise, "Dear Sir or Madam" is acceptable. Some job-hunters prefer to use "Good Morning!"

Your letter should begin by making reference to the ad. Cite the title of the position, name of the publication, and its date.

The next paragraph should state that your resume is enclosed and then provide a two- or three-sentence overview of your background as it pertains to the requirements listed in the ad.

The closing paragraph should state that you hope to hear back from the company or will be calling to follow up.

Be sure the letter is dated, and type it on the same stationery you used for your resume.

Here's the cover letter Jack Bartello would have written for answering the following ad:

SALES MANAGER

Manufacturer of polymers seeks Sales Manager for New England region. Successful candidate will have extensive experience selling to distributors, an outstanding record of increasing sales, and a B.S. in Chemistry or Chemical Engineering. Excellent salary and incentive program, comprehensive benefits, and company car. Send resume with earnings history to Box L45, Globe Office, 135 Morrissey Blvd., Boston, MA 02107. Equal opportunity employer.

Jack P. Bartello
115 Navarre St.
Hyde Park, MA 02136
(617) 361-0576

December 18, 1993

Box L45
Globe Office
135 Morrissey Blvd.
Boston, MA 02107

Dear Sir or Madam:

This is in response to your advertisement for a Sales Manager in the December 12 issue of *The Boston Sunday Globe*.

As the enclosed resume indicates, I have a track record of success in sales management as well as selling chemical products to distributors in the New England states. I hold a B.S. degree in chemistry.

I would like to interview for this position and look forward to your reply.

Very truly yours,

Jack P. Bartello

When a company identifies itself in an ad, you'll gain a reader's immediate interest—plus distinguish your response from the swarm of replies—if you can begin your letter by citing a recent news item on the company. Here, reference publications in your library, such as *Standard Rate and Data Service Business Publications Directory, Reader's Guide to Periodical Literature, Business Periodicals Index, Business Index, F&S Index,* and *Infotrac* will tell you when a company was written up by a magazine or newspaper, including the date of publication.

Had the above advertiser identified itself in its ad and had Jack Bartello been able to find a recent article on the company, his response could have been as follows (assuming the ad instructed applicants to respond to a particular individual):

Dear Dr. Aslanian:

It was with great interest that I read the recent New York Times article about your company's breakthrough in polymer manufacturing. The new opportunities and markets that this technology presents makes me especially interested in interviewing for the Sales Manager position that was advertised in the December 12 issue of The Boston Sunday Globe.

As my enclosed resume indicates, I have a track record of success in sales management as well as selling chemical products to distributors in the New England states. I hold a B.S. degree in chemistry.

I will call you shortly to discuss scheduling a time to meet.

Very truly yours,

Jack P. Bartello

Cover Letter for Sending an Unsolicited Resume to a Company

When sending an unsolicited resume to a potential employer, it's best to write to the manager who has the authority to hire you. If you know who this person is, write to him by name and title.

Mr. John F. Geer
National Sales Manager
Claude/Louie Polymer Co.
100 Summer St.
Boston, MA 01354

Dear Mr. Geer:

The following are alternatives, but they'll be less effective:

National Sales Manager
Claude/Louie Polymer Co.
100 Summer St.
Boston, MA 01354

Dear Sir:

or

Personnel Department
Claude/Louie Polymer Co.
100 Summer St.
Boston, MA 01354

Dear Sir:

The letter should begin by briefly summarizing your background and stating your most significant accomplishment in relation to the type of position you're seeking.

The next paragraph should explain that you're writing to the company because you'd like to arrange an interview and that your resume is enclosed for this reason.

The closing paragraph should state that you hope to hear back from the company or will be calling to follow up.

The cover letter Jack Bartello would have written for sending companies an unsolicited resume is as follows:

Jack P. Bartello
115 Navarre St.
Hyde Park, MA 02136
(617) 361-0576

December 20, 1993

Mr. John F. Geer
National Sales Manager
Claude/Louie Polymer Co.
100 Summer St.
Boston, MA 01354

Dear Mr. Geer:

My background is in the chemical industry, with a track record of success as a sales manager, sales trainer, and key account sales representative. For a manufacturer of industrial chemicals, I increased sales 75% within a 2-year period of time.

I would like to arrange an interview with you and have enclosed my resume for your review.

I will call you in a few days to follow up.

Very truly yours,

Jack P. Bartello

There are three instances when it's acceptable, but not recommended, to send an organization a resume without a cover letter: (1) when you're on close terms with someone at a company and he's expecting to receive your background (here, a handwritten note will suffice); (2) when contacting an employment agency; and (3) when answering a blind box ad.

The Video Resume

Due to greatly improved videotape technologies and lower equipment and production costs, the video resume is now appearing in job-hunting. This new method for generating interviews is a mock interview that's been taped. The approach is still in its infancy and there's a good deal of resistance to it, however.

Many employers consider the video resume to be pretentious. Also, few have the necessary equipment for viewing tapes in their office. And taking tapes home is inconvenient. Thus you can't expect to have great success with a video resume. However, if you feel that this method of obtaining interviews will give you a leg up on the competition and you want to use it, here are guidelines to follow:

Don't produce the tape yourself; have it professionally prepared in a studio. For companies to contact, see the *Yellow Pages* under "Video Production Services."

Before doing the taping at a studio, prepare and rehearse your script at home. It's best to first practice alone, then role-play with another person. A 10-minute tape will suffice. Be sure you're asked questions that will enable you to give a good overview of your background and, especially, discuss your key strengths and accomplishments. Section Two of this book, "The 160 Questions Interviewers Ask and How to Answer Them," will be of much help in this regard.

When you go to a studio for taping, have the interview take place in an office setting and be sure that the person who's interviewing you is off-camera and sounds professional. You can either be standing or sitting behind a desk. Dress as you would for an actual job interview.

When the taping is completed, critique your work. Look for unclear speech, repetitious words and phrases, and any mannerisms or gestures that convey nervousness. You must appear relaxed and confident and communicate effectively. If necessary, repeat the interview until you're completely satisfied with it.

Don't mail your video resume to a potential employer without first having obtained permission to do so. When you send your tape, also enclose a cover letter and your written resume. Then follow up with a phone call a few days later.

You'll have the best chance of success with a video resume if you're pursuing a position that requires an outstanding appearance and personality and you have both of these features. Usually, these will be positions that require extensive public contact.

References

It's important to line up your references before going on interviews. Most companies will want to check your background before extending an offer, and you could be asked for references at any time. The individuals that companies will prefer to talk with will be your former managers.

Before deciding to offer someone's name, speak to the person first. Not only is this courteous, it also provides the opportunity to explain how you'll be presenting yourself. In addition, you want assurance that this person's comments will support the claims you'll be making, especially about your strengths and accomplishments. Giving these people a copy of your resume will be invaluable in this regard.

If you're unemployed, always speak with your previous manager. He's likely to be contacted whether or not you provide his name. It's essential that the two of you concur on why you left the company.

If you're in doubt about the remarks a manager will make, ask what he plans to say. If you feel he's being unfair, say so and try to resolve your differences.

If you have reason to believe that a manager's comments will differ from what he tells you, you can verify this by having a friend pose as a recruiter or potential employer and call him to perform a reference check.

When you're on close terms with the people providing you with references, advise them of all the interviews that appear promising and the companies they should expect to hear from. Most important, tell them about a position's responsibilities and which of your strengths and accomplishments to highlight. This will ensure that their comments substantiate your qualifications. Also, ask these people to call you once they've spoken with a company. You want to know where you stand with your interviews, what kinds of questions are being asked about you, and if these questions follow a particular pattern. If a pattern exists, and it expresses concern about a specific part of your background or presentation, you'll know where you need to make improvements in your interviewing.

If an interviewer tells you that he wants to contact a particular manager and you're certain that his remarks will be unfavorable, there's a way to minimize their impact:

First, advise the interviewer that the comments won't be favorable and explain why. A reason frequently offered and accepted is that there was a personality conflict. Then provide the names of two other managers at the company, or the names of two individuals with whom you worked closely, who will vouch for the high caliber of your work. Their statements will neutralize the poor reference.

If you're asked to fill out an application that requests the names of your previous managers and you know that one of them will comment adversely, you're in a difficult situation. You want to volunteer this information only when you're positive that the manager will be contacted. Bringing up this matter prematurely will give reason for concern. Omitting this part of the application will arouse suspicion. And refusing to fill out the form altogether will antagonize the interviewer.

Complete the application, but ask the interviewer to advise you when he's about to check your references. Although there's no guarantee he'll oblige, the chances are good that he'll do as requested, especially if you're currently employed. It's at this time that you'll explain that there's a poor reference and give the names of additional people to contact.

Initially Contacting the Personnel Department

Considerable emphasis has been placed on (1) writing to the manager who has the authority to hire you and not to the personnel department, and (2) communicating your background via a letter instead of a resume.

There's an exception to note, however: If you're seeking an entry- or junior-level position and are open to a variety of jobs, it's advisable to send your resume to personnel. Openings might exist anywhere in a company, and this department can direct your background to the appropriate hiring manager(s).

When you write to personnel, it isn't mandatory to address a particular individual by name and title, although that would obviously be preferred.

If your resume contains negative points that might cause you to be screened out, it's best to write a letter. The letter should also be sent to a specific person by name and title, not to the "Personnel Department," "Employment Department," or "Employment Manager."

The Order in Which You Implement Strategies

Once you've decided which strategies to use, looking for a job resembles a "numbers game." You never can be sure which interview will culminate in an offer. You also can't predict the strategy that will produce this interview.

As a result, you want as many interviews as possible. Therefore, don't limit your efforts to any one strategy. Use the *combination* that best suits your objective and needs.* Also implement the strategies in the order in which they'll generate interviews the

---

* Using multiple strategies is especially important for senior-level job-seekers because the time it can take to find a new position can be as much as one month for every $10,000 of income being sought. As income approaches the $60,000 level, however, the incremental time that's needed greatly decreases.

quickest. One strategy requires special comment, no. 22, "Employment Agencies:"

If you'll be sending companies a broadcast letter, don't contact employment agencies until two weeks after the letters have been mailed. An agency might conduct its own mailing on your background and it won't present your qualifications nearly as convincingly. If a manager receives a mailing before your broadcast letter, he could make the decision not to interview you and ignore your correspondence when it arrives.

In the event that you see an agency ad that interests you, immediately call to make an appointment. When you meet your agency representative, tell him that this is the only position you want him to pursue. Explain that you've written to many companies and don't want your background to be presented to any other organizations at this time, especially through a mass mailing. If you need further assistance in the future, he'll be available to you.

Short-Term Positions as a Preliminary to Permanent Employment

Companies sometimes hire people on a short-term or part-time basis and then create permanent positions for them. Although looking for employment in this fashion isn't a job-search strategy per se, you should be aware of its possibilities.

This approach is often effective for secretaries, bookkeepers, and individuals who perform general office tasks. There are many employment agencies that specialize in temporary positions for these kinds of job-seekers, and they are listed in the *Yellow Pages* under "Employment Contractors—Temporary Help."

This short-term approach can also be of use to the senior-level job-seeker who wishes to work for a company on a consulting basis. Today, due to the emphasis on cost reduction and downsizing, more and more companies are hiring managers and executives for interim assignments.

The best way to secure such a position is through personal contacts. There are recruiting firms, however, that specialize in short-term assignments, and they usually concentrate in specific industries or fields. You can purchase a list of these companies from Kennedy Publications, 2 Kennedy Way, Fitzwilliam, NH 03447 ([800] 531-0007).

The Long-Distance Campaign

The discussion on the 30 job-search strategies has always pointed out when an approach would be effective for relocating to a particular part of the country. This objective, however, presents a certain obstacle: It will be expensive for companies to meet you, so fewer will arrange interviews.

There's a way to eliminate this financial concern. First, identify the potential employers in the geographic area of your choice. Next, obtain the names and titles of the hiring managers. Then send each person a broadcast letter that concludes by stating: "I will be in (the location) the week of (month, date) to conduct interviews. If you would like to arrange an appointment, please contact me at your earliest convenience." With the elimination of the expense factor, a greater number of companies will contact you for interviews.

Two weeks after you have sent the letters, you'll have the results of the mailing. On the basis of the interviews that have been arranged, you'll decide whether or not to take the trip. If you decide against it, advise the companies that have scheduled appointments with you that the trip must be postponed. A company might be so interested in meeting you that it will fly you out at its own expense at your earliest convenience.

When there's a small number of potential employers, conclude the letter as follows: "I will be in (the location) the week of (month, date) to conduct interviews. I will call you in a few days to see if we can arrange a time to meet." Since you'll be sending out only a few letters, you can afford the time and expense of this call. Not only will it increase your number of interviews, it will also provide the opportunity to develop leads and referrals.

The Telephone Interview

Many interviewers like to discuss applicants' backgrounds on the phone before arranging personal meetings with them. This is frequently the case with senior-level and technical positions and always when applicants are located out of town. You must therefore be prepared to receive a phone call at any time.

It's a good idea to keep a pen, some writing paper, and a copy of your resume by one or two phones in your home. This way, you'll be prepared for a call when it comes and will be able to take notes. Make sure you get the correct pronunciation and spelling of the name of the individual who's calling you along with his correct title.

If you find that you need a moment to collect your thoughts and refocus your attention at the time that a call comes, ask the interviewer to excuse you for a moment while you shut the door.

When you return, the interviewer will most likely tell you something about the position he has to fill. Before he starts to ask you questions, try to find out more about the job. Ask the interviewer to elaborate on one or two points he's already made, or ask him to describe the position's most important responsibilities and duties. The more information you can get, the more knowledgeable you'll be about the position and, in turn, the better equipped you'll be to bring forth those parts of your background that are the most pertinent to the company's needs. Your goal, of course, is for this telephone interview to lead to a face-to-face meeting.

Telephone Service

The last thing you would want to have happen is to lose interviews because company representatives were unable to reach you on the phone. Make sure your telephone will always be answered, day and night. If no one is going to be home during certain hours, buy an answering machine or arrange for an answering service.

Retail Outplacement Firms

Also known as *career marketing firms* and *executive marketing firms*, these companies are very controversial. Their numbers are growing rapidly, and they attract most of their clients through advertising their job-hunting services in the classified section of Sunday newspapers. A few of the larger firms advertise as well in *National Business Employment Weekly* and the Tuesday edition of the *Wall Street Journal*.

Some job-hunters realize great success working with these firms. Many more experience mediocre results. And a small percentage end up suing for refunds, asserting that they received shoddy assistance in return for their money and that they were promised many things that weren't delivered. Should you decide that you want to find a firm or individual to help you with your job search, your challenge will be to identify the right organization or person to work with.

Retail outplacement firms provide the following services, although very few offer this complete range: testing to identify a client's strengths, weaknesses, interests, and personality traits; establishing job and career goals; providing a list of employers and recruiters to contact; preparing resumes, cover letters, and broadcast letters, including handling their mass mailing; tailoring letters in response to job advertisements; assisting in interviewing techniques, sometimes including videotaped sessions; counseling on how to get the types of interviews desired (the focus often being a resume-mailing or letter-writing campaign, networking, and cold-calling on the telephone); providing consultation after each interview to evaluate the meeting as well as plan the next step to take; negotiating salary and benefits; and offering a telephone answering service and/or a temporary office. Some firms also contract to work with a client for several years after the new position has been found. Here, they'll offer assistance in matters such as salary reviews, performance appraisals, and evaluating future job offers.

It's important to understand that a retail outplacement firm—unlike an employment agency and an executive search firm—*will not arrange interviews for you with prospective employers*. It will show you how to do this yourself. In addition, the firm will charge you a fee that can range from a few hundred dollars to over $10,000, depending on the scope of services you sign up for and what your income level is. Some firms will require the fee to be paid in advance. Others will allow you to pay in stages as the firm performs additional work for you; however, you will have first signed a contract obligating you to pay the future installments. Additionally, this fee will not be contingent on successful results. The firm will be charging you for its time and knowledge of the employment field. If the word "guarantee" is ever used, make sure you understand exactly what's being promised and that this promise is in writing. Never rely on anything that is said orally.

How to Proceed

If you want to work with a retail outplacement firm, here are important matters to consider in order to make a sound decision concerning which organization to use:

First, determine what kind of assistance you need and want, and how much money you're willing to spend.

Second, check out a firm before you become a client. Although there are many competent firms in this field, there are also those that have limited knowledge and ability as well as little interest in helping you. Many firms have been known to close up shop shortly after commencing business. Others have been forced to cease operations due to a flood of client complaints, litigation, and the resultant bad publicity.

Always find out how long a firm has been in business. In addition, it's a good idea to check with the local Better Business Bureau, the Chamber of Commerce, and the consumer protection division of the State Attorney General's Office to see if any complaints have been filed.

In your search for top-flight assistance, also try to find people who have been clients of the firm you're considering and get their opinions as to its capability. Calling references provided by the firm will be less reliable.

Another measure to take is to find a firm that's a member of a professional association in the retail outplacement industry. Two groups that are widely known are the International Association of Counseling Services and the International Association of Career Consulting Firms. Although members of these organizations are not being endorsed by this book, they are certainly firms to consider. If you write these organizations, they'll send you a list of member firms in your geographic area. Understand, however, that some of the best outplacement firms don't belong to an industry organization and some of the most competent individuals providing these services work independently and out of their own homes.

To identify retail outplacement firms, you can also order a copy of *The Directory of Outplacement Firms* from Kennedy Publications, 2 Kennedy Way, Fitzwilliam, NH 03447 ([800] 531-0007). In addition, these organizations appear in the *Yellow Pages* under "Outplacement Consultants" and "Personnel Consultants." Some may also list themselves under "Career & Vocational Counseling."

When assessing a firm, always meet with the actual individual who will be working with you. It's very possible that the initial person you speak with is just a salesman, whose responsibility is to present the firm in glowing terms and sign you up as a client. Always ask what his function is. When you're meeting with the people who will be assisting you, make sure that the chemistry is right—that you feel comfortable with them and have an excellent rapport—and that they have the qualifications you're looking for. Find out how long they've been doing this type of work and what their educational and work backgrounds are. Also ask what their success rate has been, how long they think it will take you to find the position you want, and what their projection is based on.

Be sure you understand the specific work the firm will do for you and what work you will have to do yourself. For example, will the firm provide a list of employers to contact, including name and title of the proper individual, along with company address and telephone number? Or will the firm just give you a list of companies in the industry of your choice or show you how to obtain this type of company information at the library? What kind of counseling will you be given and will it be on an individual basis or in a group setting? Will the firm handle a mass mailing of your resume or a letter-writing campaign, or will you have to do this work yourself? Use the list of services stated earlier as a guideline for questions to ask about what services you'll be receiving.

Last, have the firm put in writing exactly what it's going to do for you, what the timetable is for these services, how long a period of time they'll be available to you, the business hours that the firm's personnel will be available to you, and what the total cost of the program will be. Again, don't rely on anything you're told that's not in writing.

When looking for professional help with your job search, you'll most likely meet individuals who are called "career counselors" and "career consultants." Here's the difference between the two.

Career counselors have advanced degrees in fields such as psychology, counseling, or social work. Their focus is often on establishing job and career goals through administering tests and exercises to identify a client's strengths, weaknesses, personality characteristics, and interests. They often have less expertise in the details of job-hunting, although they'll be able to give you useful direction in this area. Some of these individuals may even be licensed by a state agency or certified by a state or national organization, such as the National Board for Certified Counselors or the National Career Development Association. If you write these organizations, they'll send you a list of their members in your geographic area.

Career counselors usually cost between $30 and $75 an hour; however, in major metropolitan areas their fees can be in the $100-an-hour range. Often these counselors work for colleges, universities, and community mental health centers; some, though, are self-employed. They seldom work for retail outplacement firms. Career counselors can be found in the *Yellow Pages* under "Career & Vocational Counseling."

Career consultants, on the other hand, will usually lack related academic training and will place less emphasis on testing, assessment, and goal-setting. Their strength and focus will be on showing you how to set up interviews and get offers, the crux of job-hunting. Most of these individuals will have gained their expertise through working in the employment agency business, in the executive search field, or in the personnel departments of companies. Their lack of related education and a certification should not be interpreted to mean that they're less qualified than career counselors. In fact, the opposite is often the case, especially when it comes to developing and implementing highly creative and effective job-hunting campaigns. Individuals and firms can be found in the *Yellow Pages* under "Outplacement Consultants" and "Personnel Consultants." A few may also advertise under "Career & Vocational Counseling."

SECTION TWO

"What will interviewers ask me, and what are the best answers I can give them?"

THE 160 QUESTIONS INTERVIEWERS ASK AND HOW TO ANSWER THEM

An interviewer has one objective: to decide whether or not you should be made an offer. He'll arrive at his decision by asking you a multitude of questions and evaluating your responses.

He'll examine your educational background and work history to determine if you have the technical qualifications the position requires. Of all the criteria he'll assess and weigh, none will be more important than your strengths and accomplishments. Your strengths establish your ability to perform the job and your accomplishments document those strengths. In addition, past performance is the best indicator of future performance.

An interviewer will also ask you questions to investigate a host of other factors, such as your level of motivation, values, attitudes, and personality. His purpose will be to learn if you're the right type of person for the job, what your potential is for promotion, and if you'll fit into the company environment.

This emphasis on an interviewer's questions and your responses to them isn't meant to diminish the important role that chemistry can play in the hiring decision. This factor often carries as much weight as an applicant's ability to perform the job, sometimes even more.

Unfortunately, there's nothing you can do to *create* chemistry—it's either there or it isn't. But there's a great deal you can do to prepare for your interviews, so that you'll provide the best responses possible when being evaluated by potential employers. This is the purpose of this section.

Following are 160 questions you can expect to be asked, and you should have ready answers for them when you go on your interviews.

List of Questions

Questions Concerning College Experience

Why don't you have a college degree?

Why did you choose the college you attended?

How well did you do in school?

What's your most memorable experience from your college days?

What have you done that shows initiative and motivation?

If you had college to do all over again, what changes would you make?

How did you happen to select your major?

What courses did you like the most? The least?

What were your extracurricular activities?

How much of your education did you pay for? How?

What did you do during the summers?

How has college prepared you for this job (field)?

What do you think it takes to succeed in this job (field)?

Why do you think you'll like this job (field)? Why do you think you'll do well in it?

Personal Questions

How would you describe yourself?

What does "success" mean to you?

What does "failure" mean to you?

What do you want to accomplish in your life?

If you didn't have to work for a living, how would you spend your time?

What are your long-term goals? (also a work-related question)

Have you recently established any new objectives or goals? What are they? (also work-related questions)

What are your personal strengths?

What are your personal weaknesses? Are you doing anything to try to correct them?

What kind of physical condition are you in?

What do you do to stay in good shape?

Are you willing to take a drug test?

Have you had any serious illnesses or injuries? What? When?

What do people criticize about you?

What do you criticize about others?

What are your pet peeves?

What are your biggest personal accomplishments? Why were you able to attain them?

What are your biggest personal failures? Why did they occur?

What have you done to prevent them from recurring?

What's your best friend like? What kind of work does he do? How are you similar and dissimilar to him?

Are you involved in any community activities? Which ones? Why these?

How do you spend your spare time?

What kinds of books do you read? What's the last book you read?

What type of personality is the most difficult for you to get along with?

What types of people have the most difficulty getting along with you?

What do you think of me?

What else should I know about you? (also a work-related question)

Is there anything you don't want me to know about you? (also work-related)

Tell me about yourself. (work-related as well)

Questions Regarding Your Work Life

How did you happen to arrange an interview with this company?

How long have you been looking for a position?

Why are you interviewing at this time? (Why are you looking for a job?)

What do you know about this company?

What other kinds of positions are you interviewing for? With which companies?

Has anyone made you an offer yet? If so, why haven't you accepted it? If not, why not?

What do you know about this position?

Why do you want this position?

What don't you like about this position?

What do you like about this company? What don't you like about it?

What do you want from a job? What's the most important? The least important?

Are you a self-starter? If so, give an example.

What motivates you? (also a personal question)

Can you motivate other people? What techniques do you use?

What is (was) your boss's title and what are (were) his responsibilities?

What are your professional strengths?

Don't you think you're overqualified for this position?

You're overqualified for this job (have too much experience for this position). Why do you want it?

What are your professional weaknesses? What have you done to try to improve yourself in these areas?

You don't have the experience (background) (education) that this position requires. Why should we hire you?

I'm concerned about your lack of . . .

What are your biggest professional accomplishments? Why were you able to attain them?

With all your accomplishments, why isn't your salary higher?

What are your biggest professional failures? Why did they occur? What have you done to prevent them from recurring?

Have you ever been fired? Why?

What are the difficult problems you've encountered in your previous jobs? How did you solve them?

If you could start your career all over, what changes would you make?

*Did you institute any new systems, procedures, programs, or poli-
cies at your previous employers?*

Did you take any risks? If so, what were the results?

*How good are you at anticipating problems versus reacting to
them? Give an example.*

Are you a creative problem-solver? Give an example.

How do you go about making important decisions?

*What could your company (department) have done to be more
successful?*

*How well do you work under pressure? Under deadlines? Under
close supervision? With no supervision?*

*How well do you relate with superiors? With subordinates? With
people at your own level?*

What kind of management philosophy do you have?

Are you a good manager? Give an example.

Tell me about the best boss you ever had. Tell me about the worst.

*How would you feel about having a younger man (woman) as a
boss?*

*How would you feel about working with an alcoholic? With a gay per-
son? With minorities?*

Have you ever hired people? What do you look for?

Have you ever fired people? Why? How?

How do you rate yourself in your job?

*How much time would it take you to make a significant contribu-
tion at this company? Why that amount of time?*

*How long do you plan on staying in your next position? Why that
amount of time? What do you see yourself doing next?*

*What kind of position do you want to have in 1 year? In 5 years?
In 10 years? Do you think you'll attain these goals? Why?
How?*

*How long do you plan to stay with your next employer? Why that
amount of time?*

*After having been with the same company for so many years, don't
you think it would be difficult to adjust to another?*

After having had so many jobs in such a short period of time, why

*should we expect you to stay with us for any length of
time?*

*Do you think your career has progressed as fast as it should have?
Why not?*

*What salary are you looking for? How much do you want to be
earning in 5 years? In 10 years?*

How do you feel about travel? About relocation?

*What did you like the most about your previous positions? About
your previous companies?*

*What did you like the least about your previous positions? About
your previous companies?*

Why did you leave your previous company (companies)?

Why should we hire you?

Additional Questions for Women

These questions are actually illegal, as set forth by the Equal
Opportunity Employment Commission. Yet they are sometimes
asked, and women should be prepared to answer them.

*Do you plan on getting married? If so, how will this affect
your career?*

*Do you plan to have (more) children? If so, how will this affect
your work situation?*

How do you feel about supervising men?

How do men like working for you?

How does your husband feel about you working?

What would you do if your husband were transferred?

Guidelines to Consider

When formulating responses to these questions, keep your
answers brief and to the point. One or two sentences will usually
suffice. A succession of long-winded replies will just bore an interviewer.

There are also no "right" or "wrong" answers. A response that will make a favorable impression on one interviewer might not appeal to another. Some of these questions, however, afford hidden opportunities to convey qualifications. Others have disguised purposes or present certain difficulties. There are ways to shape your responses to these questions—by addressing particular topics or bringing forth specific kinds of information—that will enable you to make a favorable impression on all interviewers you meet. Here are guidelines to follow:

Questions Concerning College Experience

An interviewer will ask about college experience only if you're in the early stages of your career. The further along you are, the less emphasis he'll place on your academic background. For senior-level positions, questions concerning education will usually be omitted.

If asked about your college days, discuss academic topics and extracurricular activities that demonstrate leadership qualities or relate to your chosen field. Substantiate your early seriousness of purpose and commitment to your career. Don't portray college as having been a social experience.

Why don't you have a college degree? If you didn't complete your studies or attend college at all, an explanation most interviewers will accept is that you lacked the necessary funds or had to go to work in order to support others.

What's your most memorable experience from your college days? Tell an interviewer about an experience that is career-oriented. Never say, for example, that this is where you met your spouse.

If you had college to do all over again, what changes would you make? The changes should be ones that would better prepare you for your occupational choice. Don't say, for example, that you would attend a coeducational school or go to a college in a city versus a rural area.

How did you happen to select your major? Hopefully, your major will pertain to the position you're interviewing for, and you therefore selected it because it would prepare you for the type of work you want to do.

How has college prepared you for this job (field)? Other than taking courses that pertain to the career you've chosen, mention activities you've participated in that have prepared you as well. If necessary, explain how these activities relate to the job or field you've selected.

Personal Questions

Since an interviewer's only interest is whether or not you should be made an offer, include in your responses to personal questions information that will convey your ability to perform the job.

How would you describe yourself? Mention attributes that substantiate your qualifications for the position. Also state the important role that your work plays in your life plans.

What does "success" mean to you? What does "failure" mean to you? What do you want to accomplish in your life? and *What are your long-term goals?* Part of your response should be career-oriented. For example, "I want to hold a senior management position where I can impact a company's profitability and growth, as well as be an excellent provider for my family and play a key role in my community."

Have you recently established any new objectives or goals? What are they? This is an opportunity to demonstrate your motivation, desire to grow, and interest in improving yourself, professionally as well as personally. Be sure you have new objectives and goals to discuss. Include some that pertain to your work life.

What are your personal strengths? and *What are your biggest personal accomplishments? Why were you able to attain them?* Mention some strengths and accomplishments that convey your qualifications for the position.

What's your best friend like? What kind of work does he do? How are you similar and dissimilar to him? Because people often resemble their close friends, the first two questions probe "what you're really like." The last question is a disguised version of *How would you describe yourself?* It'll be beneficial if the discussion about this friend, especially your comparison to him, depicts you as the type of person the company is looking to hire.

Are you involved in any community activities? Which ones? Why these?; *How do you spend your spare time?*; and *What kind of books do you read? What's the last book you read?* These questions are opportunities to build rapport with an interviewer by relating interests you have in common. If no mutual interests have surfaced during the course of conversation, make note of the pictures on the office walls and any personal objects on the interviewer's desk. They might reveal hobbies the two of you enjoy. Throughout the interview you'll have chances to initiate discussions along these lines.

What type of personality is the most difficult for you to get along with? and *What types of people have the most difficulty getting along with you?* Aside from examining personal qualities, these questions investigate how compatible you'll be with the manager and how well you'll fit into his department and the company. Use your judgment, and respond in a way that will advance your candidacy.

What do you think of me? This is a difficult question. It's often designed to see how direct or diplomatic you are. Never say anything that might offend an interviewer.

Is there anything you don't want me to know about you? Don't fall for this question! Never volunteer a weakness or negative point. You have no "skeletons in the closet."

Tell me about yourself. This question, which appears as a request and is often asked at the beginning of an interview, gives many job-seekers considerable difficulty. It's perhaps the best opportunity to instantly establish your qualifications. Briefly summarize your work experience, and conclude with a discussion about your most important strengths and accomplishments.

Questions Regarding Your Work Life

How long have you been looking for a position? If you've been looking for an extended period of time, be ready to explain why you haven't received offers or accepted one.

Why did you leave your previous company (companies)? and *Why are you interviewing at this time?* Unless you were fired or laid off, it's because you're looking for more responsibility, a better opportunity, a greater challenge, or increased income. It's never, for example, because you recently had a falling out with your boss or were passed over for a promotion. You're looking for a job for positive reasons, not for negative ones. If you were fired or laid off, tell the truth. An interviewer will respect your honesty. Then explain the circumstances under which this occurred and what you learned from the experience. Turn the negative into a positive!

What other kinds of positions are you interviewing for? With which companies? Be sure your other interviews are for a similar position. This will demonstrate a well-defined objective. If you're considering a variety of positions, an interviewer might feel that you have no direction and will take any job you can get.

Why do you want this position? Because of the opportunity for growth, more responsibility, greater challenge, etc. Not, for example, because the company is closer to home or has beautiful offices.

What don't you like about this position? Never mention a key part of the job. (If this is actually the case, you shouldn't pursue the position.) State an aspect that most people would object to, a part that you would even be expected to dislike.

What do you like about this company? What don't you like about it? Your response to the first question should address how you'll be able to grow professionally and further your career. Answer the second question as above.

What is (was) your boss's title and what are (were) his responsibilities? This question is sometimes asked early in an interview to prevent an applicant from exaggerating his accomplishments and contributions. Make sure your achievements don't conflict with your boss's role.

What are your professional strengths? and *What are your biggest professional accomplishments? Why were you able to attain them?* Highlight those strengths and accomplishments that are the most pertinent to the position and that will convey your ability to handle its most important responsibilities. Being able to express the reasons for your successes will also demonstrate the thought you've put into your career and how important it is to you.

With all your accomplishments, why isn't your salary higher? This is another difficult question. Your reply could be that until recently your primary concern was job satisfaction, but now you're equally interested in income. It would then be appropriate to explain that this is why you're changing jobs. Another possibility is that your current (or previous) employer has a low pay-scale, although accompanied by a generous fringe benefits package.

If you could start your career all over, what changes would you make? This question explores how much you really enjoy what you're doing. The question is also an opportunity to convey the importance you place on your career by explaining what you would have done to improve yourself.

Did you institute any new systems, procedures, programs, or policies at your previous employers? and *Did you take any risks? If so, what were the results?* These questions probe how creative and innovative you are, whether you're a leader or a follower. When these questions are asked, the interviewer is looking for an imaginative person with leadership qualities. It'll be advantageous if your answers match the profile of the type of person the company wants to hire.

How good are you at anticipating problems versus reacting to them? Give an example. Always have examples prepared to substantiate your ability to foresee potential problems and prevent them from arising. This will underscore your expertise.

How do you go about making important decisions? This inquiry is an attempt to learn how analytical and thorough you are and whether you're a team player who seeks the advice of others or if you prefer to work independently. It will be helpful if your response portrays you as the type of person the company wants to hire.

What could your company (department) have done to be more successful? This question probes your vision as well as your interest in your work and the amount of thought you put into it. Have suggestions for improvement to discuss.

How well do you work under pressure? Under deadlines? Under close supervision? With no supervision? Be sure your replies are appropriate for the conditions under which you would be working. Also, give examples to support your statements.

What kind of management philosophy do you have? Along with examining your ideas and feelings about how people should be supervised, the purpose of this question is to find out if you'll be compatible with the manager and how well you'll fit into his department and the company.

Tell me about the best boss you ever had. Tell me about the worst. These questions also investigate compatibility. In addition, they'll elicit information about the working conditions you like and dislike. Respond appropriately for the position for which you're being interviewed.

How would you feel about having a younger man (woman) as a boss? How would you feel about working with an alcoholic? With a gay person? With minorities? Although such questions are illegal, some interviewers ask them. Your answer to the first inquiry should be that it makes no difference if your boss is a man or a woman, younger or older. You're interested only in someone's capability. As far as the other questions are concerned, always try to avoid controversial topics. Again, your interest is in someone's competence.

How do you rate yourself in your job? Highly! Then explain why by describing your key accomplishments.

How long do you plan on staying in your next position? Why that amount of time? What do you see yourself doing next?; What kind of position do you want to have in 1 year? In 5 years? In 10 years? Do you think you'll attain these goals? Why? How?; and *How long do you plan on staying with your next employer? Why that amount of time?* These questions explore your motivation and career plans. Be sure you have a well-defined goal and its timetable is realistic. If your expectations for growth are unreasonable, an interviewer might feel that you'll leave the company after a short period of time. He could eliminate you as a candidate.

After having been with the same company for so many years, don't you think it would be difficult to adjust to another? No! The transition would be easy for you because you've worked with many different kinds of people, have had managers with diverse styles, and have worked under a variety of conditions.

After having had so many jobs in such a short period of time, why should we expect you to stay with us for any length of time? This is another difficult question. Your reply could be that you've just defined your career goal and believe it could be realized at this company. Another possibility is that each change was for greater responsibility and because this company appears to reward performance with promotion, you won't have to change jobs in order to advance your career.

What salary are you looking for? How much do you want to be earning in 5 years? In 10 years? These questions, especially the last two, probe the importance you place on compensation and your level of motivation. Be sure your salary objectives are realistic and won't preclude your being made the offer. How to handle salary discussions is explained in detail in Section Five, "Salary Negotiation."

How do you feel about travel? About relocation? These questions examine your commitment to your job and career. Unless you have personal responsibilities that would prevent you from traveling or relocating, you're amenable to it. Don't discourage the offer before you know how much travel is required and what the likelihood is of having to relocate. You'll have ample opportunity to find out after you've been made the offer.

What did you like the most about your previous positions? About your previous companies? Your reply should address your responsibilities, the work you performed, and how you were able to develop professionally.

What did you like the least about your previous positions? About your previous companies? Always state unimportant aspects of the position and the company. Also, mention something you don't expect to find at the position and company with which you're interviewing.

Why should we hire you? Because of your strengths and accomplishments, which demonstrate your ability to excel at the job and grow into positions of greater responsibility.

Personal and Work-Related Questions Pertaining to Your Liabilities

Regardless of the strength of your qualifications, there will be liabilities in your background. Most interviewers will ask you to talk about them.

If you don't admit to having any deficiencies, you'll demonstrate a lack of self-awareness and immaturity. You must be willing to discuss your problem areas, but there's an effective way to do so.

What are your personal weaknesses? Are you doing anything to try to correct them? What are your biggest personal failures? Why did they occur? What have you done to prevent them from recurring?; and *What are your professional weaknesses? What have you done to try to improve yourself in this area?* Never offer a list of deficiencies. Mentioning one will suffice. Also, don't tell an interviewer about a weakness that will interfere with your ability to perform the job or that could cause him to doubt your qualifications. (If you have such a problem area, you probably shouldn't pursue the position.) Instead, discuss a deficiency that will have little impact on your performance or that could even be viewed as a strength. Examples of the latter are the tendency to become overenthusiastic about one's work and allow it to interfere with personal life, or to be impatient with delays and want to complete assignments successfully, but in the least possible time.

Of equal importance, explain what you're doing to correct the liability or compensate for it. Don't let an interviewer feel that you're ignoring it. For example, suppose you have difficulty managing your time or planning your daily activities. When discussing this problem, tell the interviewer about the measures you take to improve yourself: Each night before leaving the office, you determine what you want to accomplish the next day and how much time each task will require; then you write down the steps you'll take to assure you attain your goal. By discussing a liability in this fashion, not only do you minimize its seriousness but you turn it into a strength, since you force yourself to be proficient in planning your time.

What do people criticize about you? This is another way of asking you to describe your weaknesses. Respond as above.

What are your biggest professional failures? Why did they occur? What have you done to prevent them from recurring? In addition to answering as above, try to mention a failure that took place early in your career or that's unrelated to the position for which you're being interviewed.

Your liabilities may also surface through the course of conversation. An interviewer could then make a negative comment about some past activity. Although this reproach isn't a question, it demands an immediate response. Otherwise, the objection will crystallize in the interviewer's mind and his interest in you may diminish.

Try to offset such a remark with a positive statement, or explain what you learned from the experience, how it enhanced your capability, and why you can now prevent a similar situation from occurring.

The following are three challenges job-seekers frequently encounter, with suggested responses.

Challenge	Response
"You don't have a college degree." or "You don't have the required experience."	"I have more than the equivalent in educational background." "My accomplishments demonstrate this." (Cite your accomplishments!)
"You're underqualified for the position." or "You don't have enough experience."	"I'm a fast learner.""Look at what I accomplished in my previous position in a very short period of time." (State your accomplishments!)
"You're overqualified for the position," or "You have too much experience."	"Because of the depth of my experience, I'll be able to make an immediate contribution plus bring a fresh perspective to the department."

In addition to all the questions that have been discussed, some interviewers might ask about your age, race, religion, national origin, marital/family status and plans, financial situation, a physical handicap, or if you've ever been arrested. You might take offense at some of these questions and you should know that the Equal Opportunity Employment Commission has ruled that they're illegal, since they don't pertain to the job that someone will perform or to an applicant's work life. (An interviewer may ask, however, if you've ever been *convicted* of a crime; he just can't ask if you have ever been *arrested*.)

If you're asked questions along these lines—and you don't want to answer them—you're in a difficult situation. On one hand, you're protected by the law and don't have to cooperate with the interviewer. But on the other hand, if you tell the interviewer that he's just asked an illegal question or that you don't see how his question pertains to the job that's being discussed, you'll alienate him and hurt your chances of being made the offer.

Unless you strongly object to a certain question, the best approach to take is to be tactful and answer the interviewer as good-naturedly as you can.

Additional Questions for Women

Do you plan on getting married? If so, how will this affect your career? If you're single and plan on marrying, it won't influence your career at all.

Do you plan to have (more) children? You're undecided.

How do you feel about supervising men? It makes no difference if a subordinate is a man or a woman. You're interested only in the quality of someone's performance.

How do men like working for you? You've never been told that you're any different to work for than a man.

How does your husband feel about you working? He approves.

What would you do if your husband were transferred? You would move with him. Not only will an interviewer respect your honesty, but saying anything else would cause suspicion about the stability of your personal life.

An Exercise to Conduct

When answering an interviewer's questions, *how* you say something is as important as *what* you say. Poor articulation will dilute your credibility and your replies will have little impact.

To ensure that your answers will be convincing, there's an exercise to conduct:

First, practice each response by asking yourself a question and then reciting your reply out loud. Never memorize your answers, however. You want to sound natural and spontaneous at your interviews. If you practice with a tape recorder, you'll hear how you actually sound.

Next, have yourself "interviewed" by your spouse or a friend. Be sure you aren't asked questions in any logical sequence, though, and that their order is always changed. There's no telling when an interviewer might suddenly shift direction and ask a question about a fresh topic.

Completing this exercise will enable you to develop a polished delivery with credible responses.

This exercise also provides additional benefits:

Because you'll have formulated your replies before meeting with a company, you'll know that you can't be asked a question for which you aren't prepared. As a result, you'll never get caught short for words or have to grope for answers. This will increase your level of confidence, lessen any apprehension about being interviewed, and assure that you make the best presentation possible.

The ease with which you respond to an interviewer's questions will project intelligence, poise, decisiveness, and maturity. All interviewers are impressed with these qualities. Your responses will also evidence the self-assessment you've done and the amount of thought you've put into your career. This will convey your seriousness of purpose, commitment to success, and the full effort the company can expect from you if it hires you.

The Different Kinds of Interviewers

Although all interviewers will have the same purpose—to determine if you are the person to hire—their questions will have a different slant depending on whether someone is a hiring manager, a personnel representative, an executive recruiter, or a member of an employment agency.

Your most comprehensive interview will usually be with the hiring manager. He's the person who can least afford to make a mistake in selecting you. He'll therefore want to learn about your professional capability as well as your personal characteristics. He may even want other people's opinions about your qualifications and have you interviewed by members of his staff or other managers in the company. The higher the level of the position, the more people he'll have you meet.

In order to get a better sense of your personal qualities, the hiring manager may also take you to lunch or dinner where he'll be able to observe you in a relaxed, informal atmosphere. Never mistake this for a social affair (even if your spouse has been invited along) or interpret this to mean that you've already been selected for hire. The manager will be actively evaluating you (and your spouse as well!), even though the conversation may have nothing to do with your background or the position.

Your interviews with personnel representatives will be more varied. Sometimes hiring managers will rely heavily on these individuals' assessment of you, and your background will be examined in detail. In other instances, meeting with personnel will just be a formality before being introduced to the hiring manager, and only a cursory conversation will take place.

When it comes to interviewing, the personnel department is in a rather difficult situation. Because it's responsible for filling every position in an organization, it can seldom perform an in-depth, technical evaluation. Instead, personnel representatives will usually try to get a general sense of your background. They'll look for inconsistencies that require explanation. They'll try to establish the reasons for your job changes and why you're currently interviewing. They'll also try to determine if you're the type of person who will fit into the department and the company.

Some personnel departments may have on staff or retain a psychologist who's an extremely skilled interviewer. This individual's responsibility will be to investigate factors such as your personal characteristics, values, attitudes, current objectives, and long-term goals. Although he'll have little concern for your technical abilities, his assessment of you will be crucial to the hiring manager. He may even have the authority to veto your being hired.

Executive search firms will conduct a thorough examination of your background. They're retained by their clients to identify and refer candidates who have only impeccable qualifications. Like hiring managers, executive recruiters will be interested in both your technical capability and your personal characteristics. The majority of these individuals are also highly adept interviewers. Some will even be able to conduct a technical evaluation, since they specialize in your job function or entered the search business after a career in your field or industry.

Interviews with employment agencies will be brief. Some agencies won't even need to meet you in person. Receiving your resume and then obtaining additional information on the phone will suffice for the recruiter's needs.

The Stress Interview

The majority of your interviews will be congenial and straight-forward. Only occasionally will you encounter an interviewer who will intentionally provoke you or try to make you uncomfortable. In this situation, with emotions heightened, job-seekers act instinctively and demonstrate more of their "real" personalities.

A technique sometimes used is the "stress" interview. Inter-viewers can create stress in a number of ways:

They can frequently point out your weaknesses or problem areas; constantly interrupt you in midsentence and not allow you to finish what you were saying; try to intimidate you with their greater knowledge of your field; continually disagree with you; or be generally rude, belligerent, or antagonistic. These tactics are especially effective when there are two or more interviewers evalu-ating you at the same time.

In this setting, some job-seekers become so flustered or angry that they lose control and forget how they were trying to present themselves. Others are able to maintain their composure because they understand what an interviewer is trying to achieve and the gamesmanship that's involved.

If you meet this type of interviewer, demonstrate your mettle by "rolling with the punches."

Other methods for inducing stress, as well as to observe how assertive or submissive someone is, are to seat an applicant in a wobbly or squeaky chair or so that the sun is glaring into his eyes. Since no one wants to be interviewed under these conditions, continue the conversation while moving your chair to a different location or sitting in another one. These measures always gain an interviewer's respect.

A third technique is the introduction of silences. Here, an interviewer won't say anything after you've answered his question. He'll just stare at you. Many job-seekers become anxious under this condition and grope for things to say. Sometimes they end up revealing information that they later regret.

These silences are easy to manage. First of all, they usually don't last for more than 15 or 20 seconds, so just look back at the interviewer while slowly counting to 20. You have answered his question. It's now up to him to continue the conversation.

If these 20 seconds seem like a long period of time and you want to break the silence, ask the interviewer a question.

More than anything else, an interviewer will be using a silence to test you, to see how you handle yourself. By proceeding as above, you'll always make a favorable impression and win the interviewer's approval.

A certain type of interviewer may present a difficult situation. He's the one who is very friendly, lighthearted, and casual. He'll usually start the conversation by discussing a recent news item or topic of public interest. He'll also be in no rush to change the subject and discuss the position or your background.

In this situation many job-seekers wonder when the small talk will end and when "the interview" will begin. It already has! This interviewer is just more interested in learning about your personal qualities than he is in your work experience. He's looking to see if the right chemistry exists, if you're the type of person for the job and the company. If the interviewer decides that you're not, he'll adjourn the meeting quickly.

Once this interviewer begins to examine your background, he'll repeatedly compliment you and agree with what you're saying. The purpose of this is to make you feel confident and at ease, so that you'll drop your guard and volunteer information about yourself, especially concerning your problem areas. People are always more willing to discuss their liabilities when assured that they have gained someone's respect.

If you find yourself with such an interviewer, don't be taken in by his inviting style. Understand his technique and conduct yourself accordingly.

The Group Interview

Also known as the *board interview* and the *panel interview*, this is where you're simultaneously interviewed by two or more people. The number of interviewers can run as high as six. Board and panel interviews have traditionally been used to evaluate candidates for executive, government, and academic positions. Today, however, this type of interview is on the rise, since more and more companies are hiring people to work in concert with others as part of a team effort. Here, the entire team, or several members of it, will interview a prospective employee.

Although this group interview approach isn't necessarily used to create a stressful situation, it's undoubtedly an uncomfortable setting to be in. Many people become intimidated by the number of interviewers and say very little. They clam up as if they were being interrogated.

What you want to strive for in this interview situation is a balanced conversation with an even flow of dialogue. To achieve this, ask questions, just as you would during a one-on-one interview. Also, initiate discussions along lines where you'll be able to talk about your important strengths and accomplishments, in order to advance your candidacy.

Due to this group format, it's much more difficult to establish rapport with an interviewer. An effective way to conduct yourself when answering questions, though, is to concentrate your response and eye-contact on the individual who asked the question, while being sure to glance at each of the other interviewers during the course of your reply. This will convey confidence and poise, as well as keep the entire interviewing team engaged in your response.

SECTION THREE

"Besides giving great answers, what else can I do at my interviews to make the best possible impression?"

ENHANCING YOUR INTERVIEWING SKILLS

By providing sound answers to interviewers' questions, you'll show your capability and make a favorable impression on all interviewers you meet.

Your goal, however, is greater than this: It's to make such a fine impression that you'll have several excellent offers to choose from. To achieve this, you need to take the following steps: (1) ask interviewers intelligent and well-thought-out questions; (2) research a potential employer or the industry the company is in; (3) learn about the person who will be interviewing you; (4) close the interview on a positive note by asking certain questions; and (5) have a good appearance.

Ask Interviewers Questions

Your interviews shouldn't be a one-way street with employers asking all the questions and you providing the answers. You must ask questions as well. There are several reasons why:

By taking an active role in the interview, you demonstrate the importance you place on your job and career. If you don't ask any questions, an interviewer will feel that you have little interest in your work life and the position.

Asking questions is another way to convey your capability. The questions you choose indicate your depth of knowledge of your field as well as your general level of intelligence.

Asking questions will enable you to break down the formal interviewer/job-seeker relationship, establish an easy flow of conversation, and build rapport. The matter of rapport can't be emphasized enough. Often it's as important as having the technical capability to perform the job. Since interviewers like to hire people they enjoy talking to and can relate with, the more rapport you establish, the greater the likelihood of being selected for hire.

Your questions can serve as tools to exercise control over the conversation. If there's something you want to discuss, ask the interviewer how this matter relates to the position. This automatically steers the conversation in the direction you wish. This is an especially effective technique to inform an interviewer of an important strength or accomplishment. Just ask a question about the area in which you have excelled; after the interviewer gives you his answer, tell him about your related experience and successes.

You can also use a question to divert an interviewer's line of thought. For example, if you sense he's leading up to a subject that you want to avoid, ask a question about another topic. After a lengthy exchange, the interviewer might not return to his original line of questioning.

Last, by asking questions, you'll learn that much more about the position and the company. You'll be able to make an intelligent decision whether or not this is the right job and organization for you.

If you're seeking a senior-level responsibility, it's especially important to ask questions. An interviewer will judge you as much on the inquiries you make as he will on the responses you provide to his own questions. In addition, if you don't ask questions, you won't demonstrate the initiative and leadership qualities that a senior-level position demands.

Thus, before each meeting with a company, prepare questions to ask the interviewer. These questions, however, must concern the *position* and the *company* (or *department*). Inquiries regarding issues such as salary and benefits should be deferred until after you've been made an offer.*

---

* An exception is if you're seeking a sales position. Most companies want to hire money-motivated individuals.

Questions Pertaining to the Position

Your questions about the position will fall into two categories: technical and general.

It's beyond the scope of this book to list all the technical questions. Some general ones, however, are appropriate for all positions and will always make a favorable impression on an interviewer. They are: "What are the key tasks and responsibilities of the position?" "What are the most difficult aspects of the position?" "How does the position fit into the organizational structure?" "Starting with my manager (or "Starting with your position," if appropriate), what's the chain of command?" and "What other opportunities in the company will this position lead to?"

There are other questions, but they are more sensitive and probing and might offend some interviewers. You shouldn't ask them unless you've established a strong rapport with the individual who is evaluating you or you're on a second interview. They are: "Why is this position open?" "Why are you going outside the company to fill the position?" "What are the difficulties you've had in finding the right candidate?" "What is the person doing who used to hold this position?" and (if appropriate) "Why did he fail?" and "What were his strengths and weaknesses?" If the interviewer is the hiring manager, also ask, "What is your management style?"

Questions Pertaining to the Company (Department)

Your questions regarding the company (department) will depend on how much information you already have about the organization. An interviewer will be especially impressed when your inquiries demonstrate a knowledge of his company's history, recent successes, current goals and problems, and long-term plans. When you ask questions such as, "What business is your company in?" "What are your company's products (services)?" and "What are your company's sales?," you'll convey how little thought and effort you've put into the interview. This kind of information should be obtained *prior to* the meeting by conducting research on the organization. The way to research a potential employer will be discussed shortly.

Again, there are general questions to ask: "What are the strong points about your company (department)?" "How do you see the company (department) changing in the near future?" "What are the difficulties (challenges) (problems) the company (department) is facing?" "Are you able to tell me about the most important projects the company (department) is engaged in right now?" "What can you tell me about the new products (services) the company is planning to introduce?" "What are the company's plans for growth and expansion?" "What is the company's position in the industry? Is it gaining or losing ground with its competitors?"

Just as there's an effective way to answer questions, there's an appropriate procedure to follow for asking them:

Allow the interviewer to establish the initial tone and make the preliminary inquiries. Once he's done so, ask a question. In a short while, ask another. Let your inquiries gradually build until there's an even exchange of conversation.

If you begin an interview with a barrage of questions, you'll alienate the interviewer. He'll feel that you're trying to usurp his role, and he'll conclude the meeting in short order, eliminating you as a candidate.

Another point is that not all interviewers will react favorably to your asking a lot of questions. The hiring manager and members of his staff will be the most receptive. Representatives from the personnel department will be less so.

The main responsibility of personnel representatives is to decide whether or not you should be referred to the hiring manager. For this reason they often feel that your questions interfere with their evaluation of you.

Your primary objective with personnel representatives should be to assure that they refer you to the hiring manager and don't screen you out. It's therefore best to ask them fewer questions.

Also, confine your questions to the company, since these individuals will seldom have a detailed knowledge of the position.

An exception is when you're being interviewed by a senior member of the personnel department, such as the manager, director, or vice-president. The hiring manager will often look to this individual for guidance in his selection decision, especially about your personal qualities. It's therefore appropriate to ask this person a number of questions.

Whenever a personnel representative informs you that an appointment will be arranged with the hiring manager, there's a question you should always ask: "Is there anything in particular I should know about the position or this individual?" A personnel representative has a vested interest in seeing the position filled—it's part of his job. In addition, the hiring manager could be putting considerable pressure on him to find the right candidate. As a result, he might give you valuable information, either about certain duties of the position or the type of person the manager wants to hire.

If you find yourself on a second interview with a company, feel free to ask questions that you may have postponed during the first interview due to their sensitive nature. Just as you'll be asked more penetrating questions, you should feel comfortable probing deeper as well.

During second interviews, many companies schedule sessions with several different evaluators, where you will sequentially meet people from the same department or people from different areas of the company. An excellent way to get information about a matter that's troubling you is to ask each person the same set of questions about that issue. The consistency of the responses will be very revealing.

Second interviews are also the appropriate place to ask questions about the organization's personnel policies and corporate culture. Good questions to ask include: "How would you characterize the working environment at this company?" "What do most people like about working for this company? Are there any things that people dislike?" "How does the company differ from other companies in the industry? What is the best thing about it? What is the worst?" "Have there been any layoffs in the past few years? Any reorganizations? How was this department affected (if appropriate)?" "What is the company's policy regarding performance and salary reviews?" "Are raises based on a set formula or on an individual's contribution?" "What does the company offer in the area of training and professional development programs?" and "If I wanted to take courses at night, would the company pay for them? Would the company pay for my returning to school to earn an advanced degree?"

If the interviewer volunteers information along these lines during the first interview, it means he's very interested in you. It would then be appropriate for you to follow his lead and ask these kinds of questions at that time.

If you're interviewing with a company that's privately owned, second interviews are also a good place to ask who owns the company and when the company was founded. It's best to defer questions about sales and profitability (in the event that your research didn't uncover this information) until after you've been made the offer.

Research the Company or Its Industry

It's shocking how many job-seekers go on interviews knowing hardly anything about a potential employer. By researching a company or its industry prior to an interview, you'll realize the following benefits:

First, the information acquired through research will enable you to ask insightful and penetrating questions.

Second, when you evidence through conversation that you have researched an interviewer's company, or industry, you'll immediately convey your initiative, motivation, seriousness of purpose, and commitment to your career. All interviewers are impressed with these qualities.

Third, an interviewer will usually ask what you know about his company or why you're interested in working for the organization. Your research will enable you to provide credible responses.

Last, the more knowledgeable you are about a potential employer, the more relaxed you'll be during the interview. In turn, you'll project a confident and positive attitude.

In fact, a survey taken by a leading market research firm found that not being familiar with a potential employer will make a poor impression on 75% of the interviewers you'll meet.

At the very least, you should be aware of a company's products and/or services as well as its size, either in dollar volume or number of employees. If a company is publicly owned, you should also know whether it's earning or losing money, how much, and the current trend.

An interviewer will be especially impressed when you're knowledgeable about the following: (1) who the company's competitors are; (2) how the company compares with its competition; (3) significant events that have recently taken place in the organization or in its industry; (4) any special problems the company or industry is facing; (5) measures being taken to overcome these problems; and (6) the company's prospects and plans for growth.

If you're seeking a senior-level position, it's particularly important to be knowledgeable about a potential employer. Not only will an interviewer expect you to have researched his company, but not having done so may lead him to feel that you lack the resourcefulness and motivation that a senior-level position demands.

If you're seeking an entry- or junior-level responsibility, conducting research will give you a competitive advantage over the other applicants, since most job-seekers neglect to take this step at this level.

Researching a Company

To research a company, information is available from numerous reference books at your library:

Moody's Industrial Manual, Value Line Investment Survey, Standard & Poor's Stock Reports, and *Standard & Poor's Corporation Records* contain write-ups on over 10,000 companies. *Thomas Register; Standard Directory of Advertisers; Standard & Poor's Register of Corporations, Directors and Executives—Volume 1;* and Dun & Bradstreet's *Million Dollar Directory* and *Middle Market Directory* list the products, services, sales volume and/or number of employees of over 150,000 companies.

The state directory lists companies' products and/or services, number of employees, and approximate sales volume.

If you want to learn about a company that's a division or subsidiary of a larger organization (and it doesn't appear in the above directories), there are two sources to use. *Directory of Corporate Affiliations* gives the address, type of business, name of the chief executive officer, sales volume, and number of employees for over 40,000 companies that are owned by other organizations. The subsidiary companies appear alphabetically. The name and address of the parent organization is also provided. *International Directory of Corporate Affiliations* covers approximately 30,000 companies that are owned by larger organizations (both American and foreign) located in the United States and abroad. Name, location, and type of business are provided for the subsidiary companies. Name, address, number of employees, products/services, and names and titles of key personnel are furnished for the parent organization. The listings appear alphabetically by parent organization. The parent and its subsidiary companies are also cross-indexed by type of business and geography.

If you want to learn about a company that's located outside the United States, in addition to *International Directory of Corporate Affiliations,* the following are available:

1) *Directory of American Firms Operating in Foreign Coun-*

tries. This publication lists over 3,000 U.S. companies that have over 20,000 subsidiaries and affiliates in 121 countries. Companies are grouped alphabetically by country, noting their address and type of business.

2) *Directory of Foreign Manufacturers in the United States.* Over 2,300 foreign organizations that have subsidiaries in the United States are listed alphabetically, as well as by country. A key is provided to identify the U.S. divisions.

3) *Bottin International Business Register.* Over 100,000 foreign companies are listed by geography and products/services offered.

Newspapers and business magazines continuously run articles on companies and are additional sources to consider, especially for learning about an organization's recent successes, current problems, and future plans. If you're interviewing for an executive-level responsibility, these articles may also shed light on the position the company has available. To find the appropriate publications, see *Standard Rate and Data Service Business Publications, Reader's Guide to Periodical Literature, Business Periodicals Index, Business Index,* and *F&S Index.*

Many libraries subscribe to *Infotrac,* an on-line service that provides research reports on thousands of companies. Computer printouts are available.

In addition to conducting research at the library, here are other ways to learn about a potential employer:

A company's annual report, 10-K report, and Dun & Bradstreet report will be helpful. The last will be particularly useful for learning about an organization that's privately owned.

Most large companies have house organs (in-house newsletters) that discuss current activities and future plans. Reading these publications may also give you a sense of the company's work environment or corporate culture. To find out if an organization has a house organ, call the company or look through the *All-in-One Directory,* which lists the different publications.

Ask a company's personnel, public relations, advertising, or sales department if the organization has been written up. If an article recently appeared and it was favorable, reprints will be available. In addition, these departments will be able to tell you about the company's products and services, as well as its size.

Current and previous employees are also sources to consider. These individuals may even be able to give you important "inside" information, either about the position or the type of person the manager likes to hire.

If you were referred to a company by a recruiter, he might be knowledgeable about the organization.

Recruiters from executive search firms will always have a great deal of information. Employment agency representatives, however, usually won't. In addition, you must be careful about what agencies tell you, since the people there work on straight commission and don't get paid unless the company hires you. Thus they will often present a biased assessment of a company.

If your interview is with a publicly owned company, your stockbroker might be following the organization or be knowledgeable about its industry. If not, he might be able to put you in touch with someone who is or provide you with a recent brokerage report.

The company's suppliers, customers, and competitors will always have a wealth of information, particularly about recent developments and any significant problems the organization is encountering. These individuals might be difficult to reach, though.

Researching an Industry

There's also a great deal of information available about different industries:

U.S. Industrial Outlook and *Standard and Poor's Industry Surveys* give overviews on nearly 350 manufacturing and service industries, with comments on prospects for the future. Business magazines such as *Forbes, Fortune,* and *Business Week* publish an issue near the first of each year that reports on the status and outlook for different industries. (See the *Special Issues Index* and *Guide to Special Issues and Indexes of Periodicals* for the dates of these issues.) *Standard Rate and Data Service Business Publications, Business Periodicals Index, Business Index,* and *F&S Index* will tell you which trade journals to read for any industry of your choice. The *Wall Street Journal Index* cites the editions of the *Wall Street Journal* and *Barron's* that discuss a specific industry. Last, your library may subscribe to *Infotrac,* which provides computer printouts of articles written about different industries.

In order to have sufficient time to conduct this research, try to schedule your interviews several days off. Don't let employers pressure you into meeting with them after having given you only a day's notice.

In the event that you're looking for your first job or are considering making a career change, you might also want to research the position(s) you're considering. Volume 1 of *Encyclopedia of Careers and Vocational Guidance* discusses 71 industries and fields, including suggestions for follow-up reading. *The Occupational Outlook Handbook* describes 250 occupations, including their responsibilities, educational and work experience requirements, projections for growth, and income potential. This publication also lists additional sources for information on each job category. Volume 2 of *Encyclopedia of Careers and Vocational Guidance* covers 650 occupations, including sources for further information. *The Dictionary of Occupational Titles* details approximately 25,000 jobs.

Learn About the Interviewer

Always obtain the name and title of the person who will be interviewing you. Also, try to learn something about this individual before the meeting. There's no telling what the two of you might have in common that will enable you to "break the ice" and build rapport. It could be people you both know, where you grew up, where you currently reside, a school you both attended, a company you've both worked for, or hobbies and interests. In addition, it's helpful to know the type of personality you'll be meeting. Being forewarned that someone can be hard to get along with will prepare you for a possibly difficult session.

If your appointment is with an executive, his background might be described in one of the following publications: Dun & Bradstreet's *Reference Book of Corporate Managements; Standard & Poor's Register of Corporations, Directors and Executives—Volume 2; Who's Who in Business;* or *Who's Who in America.*

The vast majority of the time, however, interviewers will not have been written up nor will you be able to learn anything about them before the meeting. Therefore, upon entering someone's office, make a point of noticing the pictures on the walls and personal objects on the desk. They might reveal interests you have in common. Throughout the interview, you'll have opportunities to build rapport by initiating discussions along these lines.

Also, many job-seekers have a false impression of their relationship with interviewers. They consider the interviewer to be in the position of strength and see themselves in a subordinate role. This causes feelings of intimidation and apprehension and makes the interview situation a difficult one.

The fact of the matter is that interviewers have qualms about these sessions as well, especially when they're the hiring manager.

First of all, a manager is under greater pressure to hire someone than you're probably aware of. In fact, the only reason he's conducting interviews is because there's something lacking in his department: He has work that must be done and no one with the required experience to do it. Until he hires the right person, his optimum performance is being held back. On top of this, his manager is constantly evaluating how well he's doing *his* job.

Second, most managers aren't skilled interviewers. They have little training in this area, and their expertise lies in performing their functional specialty, not in interviewing.

Third, most managers don't enjoy interviewing. They regard it as an intrusion on their time that prevents them from attending to their primary responsibilities. They see interviewing as downtime.

As a result, a manager *hopes* you're the person to hire. If you are, he'll be able to fill his opening and bring this burdensome and unwelcome process to an immediate and successful conclusion.

Instead of being apprehensive about being interviewed, think about all the experience you have, how well-qualified you are for the position, and how vital your background is to an employer. You're on much stronger ground than you imagine.

Closing an Interview

When an interview is over, you'll want to know where you stand with the interviewer: Did you make a favorable impression and what are your chances of being made the offer? There are several ways to determine this:

First, certain signs are obvious indications that a meeting went favorably. The interviewer schedules a second appointment. He tells you that he wants you to take some tests or meet with the company psychologist. He makes a point of introducing you to his boss or states that he wants you to meet with him or with some of the key people in the department. He speaks enthusiastically about the position and/or the company. He discusses starting salary. He asks for references. Or he concludes the interview by saying something such as, "I won't be able to finalize things for a few weeks, but if anyone makes you an offer in the meantime, call me at once."

There are questions the interviewer can ask that also indicate a high level of interest: "Do you think you'd like to join us?"

"When would you be able to start?" and "How much notice do you have to give your employer?"

In most cases, though, interviewers will have other applicants to meet and won't be that specific about where you stand. They frequently end conversations by saying, "I've enjoyed talking with you and we'll be in touch."

Job-seekers always want to know what "we'll be in touch" really means and when they can expect to hear from a company. To find out, you can ask one or two of these questions: "Do you feel I have the qualifications you're looking for?" "Is there any additional information you'd like about me?" "What is the next step?" "When do you want the new person to start?" and "When do you plan on making your hiring decision?" An interviewer's response to any of these questions will give you a better indication of your chances of being hired.

One additional question is particularly effective: "Is there any area in which you feel I fall short of your requirements?" Not only does this question probe an interviewer's level of interest, it also provides the opportunity to correct a misconception about your qualifications, should this be the case.

Another way to determine an interviewer's enthusiasm for you is to tell him that you want the job. For example, if you were to say, "I know I can meet the demands of the position, would make an outstanding contribution, and I'd like the offer," an interviewer can't be vague. He must make a statement about your chances of being hired. If he doesn't, he isn't interested in you at all.

If you decide to ask for the job, be sure the interviewer has the authority to hire you or is one of the key decision-makers. Otherwise, he'll tell you that the decision isn't up to him and he can't speak for the other parties involved. Also consider the level of the position, the number of interviews that's reasonable for such a responsibility, and the number of meetings you've had. For example, if you're pursuing a vice-presidential position, it would be inappropriate to state that you want the job after the first interview. Doing so would demonstrate naiveté as well as the tendency to make hasty decisions.

A final step that's proven effective for many job-seekers is to tell the interviewer that you're interested in the position, but you have an offer from another company and must give a decision within a few days. The interviewer's response to this time constraint will reveal his level of interest.

Appearance

If you have a poor appearance, an interview will never even get off the ground. An interviewer will give you a few minutes out of courtesy and then end the meeting.

Always be neat, clean, and well-groomed. Although all job-seekers claim to know this, it's shocking how often they forget when it comes to their own interviews. Also, dress appropriately for the position and the company. For example, what would be proper attire for a vice-presidential responsibility at a bank would be inappropriate for a creative job at a small advertising agency. The reverse is also true.

Your appearance will never win you the job (unless you're applying for one of those rare positions where it happens to be the most important criterion), but it can easily cost you the job.

Make sure your clothes fit well, collars aren't frayed, colors are well coordinated, shoes polished, and fingernails clean. It's best to dress on the conservative side and to select clothing that resists wrinkling. Stripes will make you look taller and leaner, while plaids will have the opposite effect. Don't wear jewelry, pins, or cuff links that indicate membership in a religious, fraternal, or service organization (unless you have advance information that your prospective manager is such a member).

Men should wear only functional jewelry and never any that would make them look feminine. A suit and tie is appropriate for most positions. Cologne should be used sparingly and hair should always be combed.

Women should usually wear a dress or suit. Large jewelry, strong perfumes, excessive makeup, and exotic hairstyles are to be avoided.

Drug Testing

Today, an increasing number of companies—large and small alike—are giving drug tests to job applicants. These tests are administered most often when the employee's safety might be at risk due to the type of work involved. If you're asked if you'll agree to take a drug test, don't refuse. The test may never be administered.

In the event that a test is scheduled, however, there are precautions to take so that you won't give what's known as a "false positive." This is where the test shows that you have an illegal substance in your system, even though you actually do not.

For several days prior to the test, avoid all foods that have poppy seeds in them as well as pain relievers, cough syrup, and gin. The ingredients in these products can indicate that you've been using an illegal drug. It's also a good idea to have flushed out your system by drinking a good deal of water for two or three days before the test.

Some companies will have you fill out a form that will tell you which over-the-counter and prescription medicines the test will be sensitive to. If a company administers a test and doesn't provide this form, though, always advise the person giving the test of any medicines you've taken during the past three weeks. Some substances can stay in your system that long, and they might produce a false positive result.

SECTION FOUR

"When I want the job, what can I do after the interview is over?"

POST-INTERVIEW ACTIVITIES

This is the part of the job-search process that most people neglect. It's also the part that the skilled job-seeker uses to convert a maximum number of interviews into offers.

Examine Your Interviews

After an interview has ended, immediately make note of all the important points that were discussed. Be sure to include the responsibilities the interviewer emphasized, the areas in which you feel you impressed him the most, and any tasks he seemed uncertain you could handle. You'll be using this information in your follow-up activity with the company.

Then study the interview to determine what changes you could have made to have enhanced your presentation. You might find that you missed opportunities to ask important questions, failed to tell the interviewer about certain strengths, accomplishments, or experiences, could have provided better answers to certain questions, or said something that made a poor impression.

Each interview should be regarded as a "dress rehearsal" for future appointments, with the company in question as well as with others. By reviewing your meetings, you'll continually sharpen your interviewing skills and make more successful presentations.

Follow Up with the Interviewer

Your next step is to send a thank-you letter to the key people you met. If you saw only a member of the personnel department, write him a note. If you were also interviewed by the hiring manager, write to both parties. In the event that you were interviewed by several people, write to all of them. Always get business cards from each person you met so you'll be sure to have the correct spelling of their names plus their titles. Mail your correspondence within the next few days, the following day if you're a junior-level job-seeker and a few days later if you're at a senior level.

There are two kinds of thank-you letters: The first is for a position you won't be pursuing, either because the interviewer volunteered that you weren't a strong candidate or the job was of no interest. In both cases, show courtesy and send the interviewer a brief note in which you express your appreciation for his time. It's best not to use the actual words *thank you*, though; you don't want to put yourself in a subordinate role.

Being courteous, however, isn't the only reason for writing this letter; a new position could arise at a future date. Also, during the process of conducting interviews, companies sometimes redefine their needs and the type of person they want to hire. This letter will make a favorable impression and ensure that you're actively remembered.

The other kind of thank-you letter is designed for interviews that went more positively and where you want to pursue the position with the hiring manager. Begin this letter by expressing how much you enjoyed meeting the manager. Then summarize the job's most important responsibilities and your pertinent strengths and accomplishments. Conclude by stating your interest in the job and the company.

This letter serves several purposes. Along with showing courtesy, it reinforces your understanding of the company's needs and your proven ability to fill them. It also provides the opportunity to present key information you may have omitted during the interview or to discuss a point that requires clarification. Most importantly, though, it allows you to keep an open line of communication with the manager. One week after writing to him, you're going to call him "to make sure he received your letter." After he tells you that he did, wait to see what he says next. The following are the responses you'll hear most often and the procedures to follow:

The manager tells you that he's decided to hire someone else

Use this as an opportunity to get feedback on your interviewing and to obtain referrals to managers at other companies. First, ask where you fell short of the manager's requirements and if you might be able to improve your presentation in any areas. Then ask for leads.

If this is a company you're extremely interested in working for, you might try calling back every four to six weeks to see if there are any new openings for which your background is better suited. This call will ensure that the manager remembers you in the event that the right position comes along. Your enthusiasm for working for the company will also serve you in good stead. If you have reservations about making this kind of follow-up call, ask the manager if you may call him periodically to check on the possibility of new positions in his department.

The manager mentions a reservation about you

Always try to counter an objection. The manager's response will indicate whether or not you were successful and if you should ask for leads at this time.

The manager states that you're a strong candidate

This is the response you were hoping for. Try to engage the manager in conversation in order to build more rapport and enhance your relationship with him.

What you choose to talk about will depend on the amount of rapport you've already established. Several topics, though, are always appropriate: You can ask a question about the position, the department, or the company. If the manager has divulged a problem he's been trying to solve, discuss your ideas for a possible solution.* If you've noted a recent business development or news item on the company, inquire about the effect it might have on the position or the organization.

The actual subject you discuss isn't that important so long as it sparks an interest in the manager. Ideally it will prompt him to suggest getting together to continue the conversation in person. (You can even make this suggestion yourself!) If you're successful in arranging this appointment, you'll have set up a second interview and gained a competitive advantage over the other applicants.

Although all managers won't schedule this meeting, this call will never be a waste of time. At the very least you will strengthen your relationship with the person who can hire you. You may also advance yourself from being one of several candidates to the leading contender.

If you have an offer from another company, always tell the manager, especially the date by which you have to give your decision. Not wanting to risk losing a qualified individual, he could expedite matters and make you the offer.

Writing this thank-you letter and placing this call are the minimal follow-up activities you should conduct when a position interests you. When you want to pursue an offer vigorously, however, and you are certain the interview went favorably, you should proceed in a slightly different fashion.

---

* Here you must be aware of two potential pitfalls: (1) offering a solution that has already been tried and that failed; (2) disclosing the extent of your ideas and risking that they'll be adopted without your being hired.

First, write the manager the appropriate letter. Next, conduct further research on his company or its industry. Then call to verify that the manager received your correspondence. After he tells you he has, advise him of your research, explain that there are questions you would like to ask, and try to set up a time to discuss this in person.*

The chances are now excellent that the manager will see you. Someone who is under consideration for hire has investigated his company and has questions to ask. It's in the manager's best interest to set up this meeting.

When you see the manager, you'll make an even more favorable impression. Your inquiries will be that much more insightful, because of the research you just conducted and due to what you learned during the first interview. In addition, since the manager has agreed to this appointment, he's indicating that you're a top candidate. You now have an opportunity to convince him to hire you, and preempt your competition.

Regardless of the amount of follow-up activity you conduct, any at all will convey your interest in the position. This will always work in your favor, since a manager's selection decision is often subjective and not based solely on an individual's technical competence. Other factors can come into play:

For example, it isn't unusual for a manager to have met several equally qualified candidates and to have difficulty determining which one to hire. Here, he may opt for the individual who has expressed the most interest in the position. This guarantees him of an enthusiastic and committed new staff member.

Demonstrating your desire for the job can help you in another way. As already discussed, most managers consider the interview-

---

* If the interview was with a company located out of town, this meeting won't be possible. In this case, call the manager, explain the research you have done, and then discuss your findings and ask the questions that you have formulated.

ing process to be a time-consuming and burdensome ordeal that interferes with their primary responsibilities. On top of this, they face three potential problems when deciding which candidate to hire:

- The person they select could reject the offer outright.
- This individual could request some time to think the offer over and then turn it down. (This would cost the manager time. He might also lose other highly qualified candidates in the process and have to start interviewing all over again.)
- This person could accept the offer but never actually start work, either because his current employer persuaded him to remain with the company or he received a better offer elsewhere. (Again, the manager would lose valuable time.)

By expressing your desire for the position, you'll relieve the manager of these concerns. He knows that if he makes you the offer you'll accept it. This gives him additional incentive to select you for hire.

For these reasons, don't hesitate to tell a manager that you want the job and ask for the offer. There's clearly no better combination in an applicant than the right qualifications and a keen interest in the position.

As a conclusion to this discussion, the following matters need to be covered.

The timing of your follow-up activity must be adjusted to the individual situation.

If a manager tells you that he isn't planning to hire someone for a month or two, or that he's uncertain about the specific experience he needs and intends to clarify this through interviewing different people, defer part of your follow-up activity. Certainly write a thank-you letter after the interview, and also call the manager one week later. During this conversation, however, limit your questions and comments and don't mention that you conducted further research. Save the majority of such a discussion for a later date, when the manager is closer to making his hiring decision. At that time your remarks will have greater impact.

As a general rule, the higher the level of a position, the more people a manager will interview, the more appointments he'll arrange with each one, and the more time he'll need to make his decision. Asking the questions that appeared in "Closing an Interview" will enable you to decide how to time your follow-up plans.

If you're being pursued by a company through an executive search firm, conduct a minimum of follow-up activity. Send a manager a thank-you letter after the initial interview, but don't call him on the phone. The search firm, on behalf of the company, made the initial contact. It's best not to disturb this momentum. Besides, the recruiter's follow-up with you will keep you apprised of where you stand.

Your follow-up activity for positions being handled by executive search firms will usually have less impact on a manager. Because these organizations are so proficient, a manager expects to find the ideal candidate, one who is both highly qualified and interested in his company and job. He'll usually withhold making an offer until he meets such a person.

If you decide to take the additional step of conducting research after an interview, understand that it will be the most effective for job-seekers who are pursuing entry- and junior-level positions or who are making a career change. In these cases, people are hired more for their potential than for the immediate contribution they'll make. You'll always demonstrate your potential by conducting this research and by the insightful questions you will ask as a result.

The main value of doing research for senior-level positions is that it's a vehicle for staying in touch with a manager. He won't be impressed by the fact that you took the time to learn more about his company; he will expect you to have done so.

Finally, many job-seekers fear that demonstrating their interest in the position will result in their receiving a lower offer. This will seldom be the case; a manager won't assume you want the job at any price.

Your primary goal should be to get the manager to make you the offer, and then you can turn your attention to obtaining the highest possible salary.

SECTION FIVE

"How do I make sure I'm offered the highest possible salary?"

SALARY NEGOTIATION

Of the many factors that job-seekers evaluate and weigh when they receive an offer, salary is by far the most important one. It's the reason why most people work and job-seekers' single greatest consideration when deciding whether or not to accept an offer. Unfortunately, many people don't know how to handle this salary issue and they accept lower offers than they need to.

When it comes to salary, there's also a conflict of interest between company and potential employee. A company is in business to make a profit and therefore wants to minimize expenses. Since salary is an expense, the company tries to keep its offers as low as possible. A job-seeker, on the other hand, is looking to make the most money he can and wants the highest attainable salary. Thus a difference of opinion can arise concerning an equitable figure, and negotiating begins.

Getting a company to increase its offer is easier than most job-seekers realize. The salary that's initially proposed is frequently designed to "test the water." Although it's an amount of money that the company believes will be accepted, it isn't the greatest possible sum. The company will agree to a higher figure if given good reasons to support it. As positions increase in seniority, organizations become that much more willing to negotiate.

The Cardinal Rule in Salary Discussions

When discussing salary, there's an approach to take that virtually guarantees successful results: *Get the company to disclose what it wants to pay before you divulge the amount you're seeking.* By adhering to this rule, you'll receive *a higher initial offer* and be able to negotiate *a further increase* from this level.

When you reveal your salary objective prematurely, you jeopardize your negotiating position. Here's why:

Whatever salary you ask for will usually become *the maximum* the company will offer. Not only will you be setting a ceiling on the amount, but the company will probably suggest a lower figure, knowing it can go to this level if necessary.

If the amount you request is significantly *below* what the company was planning to pay, your self-confidence and ability could be questioned and the company could develop second thoughts about your qualifications. It might even eliminate you as a candidate.

If the figure is too far *above* what the company had in mind, it could assume you would be dissatisfied with its offer or reject it outright. Again, you could be disqualified.

On the other hand, when the company is the first party to mention salary, you face none of these risks. In addition, the figure will be the *lowest* salary that will be offered and negotiating will be *upward* from this amount.

In the course of interviewing with a company, you'll usually be asked what salary you want. It's easy to defer this discussion. When asked during the first interview, an appropriate reply is: "I don't have a set figure in mind. I also don't know enough about the position yet." When asked after you've had more than one meeting, your response can be: "I'm extremely interested in the position but am still open on salary. It would depend on the benefits package, the opportunity for bonus or profit sharing, and offers I'll be receiving from other companies." Most interviewers will accept these replies.

If you're interviewing for a position that would necessitate relocation, it's acceptable to add that you would have to assess the cost-of-living differential.

At a certain point, though, especially when a company has decided you're the candidate to hire, an interviewer will try to pin you down on your financial requirements. He might say, for example: "Jack, we're all very impressed with you and would like to have you on board. What'll it take?"

This is the most tempting time to disclose the desired salary. Some job-seekers also interpret this question to mean that they can write their own ticket. This is seldom the case; the interviewer is only feeling them out.

Because of the potential problems of revealing the salary objective, never give an interviewer a *specific figure*. Instead, state a *range*.

There are guidelines to follow for determining this range. Most importantly, it must be realistic and in accordance with the general pay scale for the position. If you're changing careers or are planning to move to a new industry where salaries differ, you might not know what a reasonable range would be. To find out, ask people who work in the industry or speak with the appropriate executive search firms, employment agencies, or professional and trade associations. In addition, *National Business Employment Weekly* continuously publishes salary surveys on the various job functions in a host of different industries and fields. You can call or write this publication for the back issue that pertains to your specialty.

Once you've decided on your range, be sure that the spread between the high and low points doesn't exceed 10%. For example, you could be seeking between $20,000 and $22,000, between $50,000 and $55,000, or between $200,000 and $220,000. Set the low point at 5% below the salary (or upper figure in the range) that the company told you it wants to pay. For example, if the company stated $60,000 (or between $55,000 and $60,000), give a range of $57,000 to $63,000.

You must also carefully evaluate five factors, since they always influence an offer: (1) how pressing it is for the company to fill the position; (2) how enthusiastic the manager is about hiring you; (3) how competent you are in your line of work; (4) whether the company has a reputation for being a high- or low-paying organization; and (5) your current or previous salary.

In addition, geography can play a role. If you're currently working in an area where living expenses and salaries are high but are interviewing for a position where the cost of living and salaries are low, you can't expect to receive a large increase, if any at all. When companies decide on compensation, they always take this cost-of-living factor into consideration.

Finally, when giving your range, tell an interviewer about any bonus, profit sharing, or special fringe benefits you currently enjoy or a raise you're due with your current employer. Also mention offers you've already been made or are expecting to receive from other firms. These, too, influence compensation decisions.

Some interviewers won't be satisfied with being given a range and will press you for a specific figure. Unless you have reason to believe that continuing to withhold this information would be disadvantageous, don't yield. You've been told the company wants to hire you. It's now the interviewer's responsibility to name salary, not yours. Roles have changed. The company is now "the seller" and you are "the buyer."

Receiving the Offer

Once a company has extended its offer, you're in the driver's seat. This is the time to inquire about matters such as fringe benefits, travel, and relocation. It's also the time to ask questions you may have withheld because you were concerned about how an interviewer would react to them.

Two questions you should always ask are: "Is there anything you think I might not like about the position or the company?" and "Are there any areas in which you think I might encounter difficulty?" Interviewers usually paint a glowing picture of a position and their company, but both often have undesirable features. Although company representatives seldom volunteer this kind of information, they're usually candid when asked.

Once all your questions have been answered, if you're satisfied with the offer, accept it. If you're currently employed, ask for a letter confirming the details before giving your "official" acceptance and notifying your present employer. (It's a good idea to ask for this letter even if you're unemployed, especially when you're expecting several offers.)

If you want some time to think the offer over, work out a mutually agreeable date for advising the company of your decision. Although an immediate answer will be desired, it will seldom be demanded. Employers are accustomed to giving people anywhere from a few days to several weeks, depending on their level of seniority and the urgency of filling the position.

If you find that you need more time than you had originally anticipated (you could be waiting for a better offer from another company), there are two ways to handle this situation. You can ask for an extension, or you can explain that you want to discuss certain matters about the position (or the company) and schedule a meeting for this purpose. Clearly, the further away you arrange the date of this meeting, the more time you'll have obtained for yourself.

If you want the job but are disappointed with the salary, then negotiate for more money.

The procedure for negotiating will vary depending on whether the offer was made by the hiring manager or a personnel representative and whether it was extended in person or over the phone. Before discussing how to treat these variables, here's the general format for requesting an increase. It's a three-step procedure:

First, assure the individual making the offer that you're interested in the position and the company.

Next, explain that you were hoping for a higher salary and will accept an offer if the amount is increased. It's at this point that you state a specific figure. However, in accordance with all sound negotiating principles, ask for a salary that's a little above the amount you want. This will give the company room to negotiate back without your being penalized. You may also receive a pleasant surprise!

The last step is to justify the increase. The reasons you give to support it are as important as the amount of money you ask for. Base your request on *your qualifications and value to the company*, not on your personal needs. For example, never ask for an increase because you want to buy a new house, are expecting a child, or haven't had a raise in over a year. In the last case, a company doesn't want to pay for what another has been able to get away with! Moreover, it isn't to your credit that your employer passed you by.

Once you've reinforced your capability, it's appropriate to state additional reasons for deserving a higher salary.

If you think the company arrived at the amount it offered you by using your current or previous income as a base figure and automatically increasing the amount by a fixed percentage, explain that the two positions aren't as comparable as they might appear to be and why you represent greater value to this company than to the other.

If you have a higher offer from another organization but want to work for this one, advise the company of the offer and that you'll accept theirs if the offer will be increased to equal the other. In this situation, companies often match their competition or increase the initial offer, without even asking to see an offer letter.

A final possibility is to try to have your responsibilities expanded in order to warrant a higher salary.

This is the general procedure for negotiating an increase. Certain modifications are necessary depending on the circumstances under which the offer is made.

The ideal situation is when the hiring manager extends the offer in person. In this case, conduct yourself as above. However, if the manager makes the offer *over the phone* and the company is *local*, proceed in a slightly different fashion. After you've expressed that you're enthusiastic about the position and the company but that you had anticipated a higher salary, suggest coming in to discuss the offer in person. Some managers will arrange this meeting while others will prefer to negotiate at this time. The mere suggestion of this appointment, though, will put the manager in a more accommodative frame of mind.

If the hiring manager extends the offer *over the phone* and the company is located *out of town*, the negotiating will almost always be conducted during this phone call. It's only for executive-level positions that a company will fly someone in to finalize compensation. Conduct your negotiating as if the offer had been made in person.

If the offer is made by a *personnel representative*, the situation is more complex. You don't know if your salary was determined by the personnel department or by the hiring manager. You also don't know how much authority, if any, this individual has to negotiate with you. In some instances, it will be part of his job. In others, his sole responsibility will be to extend the offer and apprise the manager of your reaction to it.

When the company is *local*, advise the personnel representative of your interest in the position and the company, that you were hoping for a higher offer, and that you would like to arrange a meeting to explain why you feel an increase is warranted. He'll either negotiate with you, set up an appointment, or ask what salary you're seeking and tell you that he'll speak with the manager and call you back.

When the company is located *out of town*, proceed as above, but explain that you would like to discuss your reasons for deserving an increase. This gives the personnel representative the opportunity to negotiate with you if he has the authority to do so.

It's important to be tactful when speaking with a personnel representative. Regardless of your feelings about an offer, never be rude or say anything that might irritate him. He could be the person with whom you end up negotiating! If not, he's now your link to the manager, and how he communicates your reaction and attitude can have a significant impact on the manager's willingness to accommodate you.

There will be times when a company won't increase its initial offer. Here, try to negotiate a raise to a certain level after a three- or six-month period. You can also negotiate the following: a performance bonus, stock option, expense account, insurance policies, vacation time, company car or car allowance, club membership fees, and legal, tax, and financial planning assistance.

If you were referred to a company by an employment agency and it's your responsibility to pay the fee, ask the company to assume this expense. If the company declines, try to negotiate reimbursement after a 3-, 6-, or 12-month period. Since companies are usually amenable to the latter, always ask to be reimbursed, whether or not you're negotiating salary.

Regarding Your Current or Last Salary

What to say to interviewers when they ask about your current or last salary is one of the trickiest parts of salary discussions.

If your income is low, some employers will view this favorably because it won't cost them a lot of money to hire you. Others, however, will question your abilities.

If your earnings are high, this could preclude your being made the offer. Yet some employers might see this as validation of your capability and expertise and become that much more interested in hiring you.

Clearly, there are good reasons to tell an employer what you've been earning as well as to withhold this information.

When deciding how to handle this matter, there's also another factor to consider: Some employers will be angered by your refusal to discuss your earnings level, while others will understand that you want an offer to be based on your value to the company and not on what some other organization has been paying you.

The best approach to take is to weigh all these variables and handle questions concerning your current or last salary on an individual basis. Depending on the circumstances, you might reveal your income level to one employer but not to another.

Giving Notice to Your Present Employer

Once you've accepted an offer, give your manager reasonable notice that you'll be leaving the company. Two weeks is usually an appropriate amount of time, except for senior- and executive-level positions.

Never advise the manager in a way that could cause resentment or bitterness, regardless of how difficult it was working for him. You might need his reference at some point in the future. The two of you might also end up at the same company.

In addition, you want the opportunity to be made a counteroffer. Because companies don't like to lose valuable employees, they frequently promote people, transfer them to a different department or division, create a new position for them, or match another company's offer when given resignations. Although these "forced reassignments" and salary increases don't always prove advantageous in the long run, you still want the option of being able to consider such a proposal.

Some job-seekers use this situation as leverage to negotiate a higher offer from another company. They give notice *before accepting the offer*, with the expectation of generating a counteroffer from their current employer. Then they inform the other company of their new salary in hopes of obtaining yet another increase.

After you've arranged a starting date with your new employer, thank all the people who helped you in your search and advise them of your new position. Either call them on the phone or write them brief notes.

Index

About the Author

Born in New York City and raised on Long Island, John J. Marcus graduated from the University of Pennsylvania with a degree in sociology. For the past 25 years, he has conducted technical recruitment, executive searches, outplacement, and career counseling in Los Angeles, San Francisco, Boston, and Florida.

Mr. Marcus currently resides in Sarasota, Florida, where he is the owner of CareerCrafters, a career-counseling and resume-writing firm.